# Get Your Hero Up a Tree

## How to Write a Movie (That Doesn't Stink)

## Mark Achtenberg

ISBN: 978-1-64136-527-7
Run Amok Books, 2018
First Edition

# Praise for *Get Your Hero Up a Tree*

"Mark Achtenberg's book is a common sense, accessible approach to screenwriting, aimed at students and "young" writers. Written by a writer and teacher who is also an excellent picture editor, the book is filled with practical insights and approaches, based on examples of real films that students will know. It gives the writer a number of choices and the reasons behind them to consider in her or his own original work and does so in a way that encourages the writer to stay true to the passion of the idea and discourages a formulaic 'one way' approach."

— Lawrence Mirkin, producer on Fraggle Rock and the Jim Henson Hour—

"How to write with moving pictures has often been shrouded in a fog of conflicting advice. *Get Your Hero Up A Tree* looks clearly through to the heart of what is necessary. Follow Mark's advice and never get lost. It makes a fuck of a lot more sense than anything Robert McKee ever blabbered on about."

— Robert Mills, writer, director, founder of Radical Sheep Productions —

"This guy has been working in the biz for 20 years and he's passing on a lot of hard-won wisdom in this book. Whether you buy this book to help you achieve your screenwriting ambitions or to increase your understanding of how films work, you'll find it an enjoyable and invaluable read."

— Henry Brock, author of Vicious Dogs—

# Contents

## INTRODUCTION

As a teenager I became obsessed with photography. I discovered my father's old manual Pentax camera and learned photography the old-fashioned way. I was also obsessed with movies, watching everything I could get my hands on from the local, but limited, Blockbuster Video. One day I had exhausted the catalogue of new movies and I was lamenting the lack of good movies to watch. My mom said I should rent *The Godfather*. My initial response was typical of a young person—why would I watch an "old" movie? My mom persisted (apparently, my grandfather walked out of the movie during the horse head scene) and I eventually caved in and rented the movie. It put the zap on my brain. From there I went down the rabbit hole of classic films.

A few years later I started my degree in literature and, at some point, saw Spike Lee's *She's Gotta Have It* and the zap was on again. Reading about the film, I was inspired by Lee's conviction that anyone should be able to make a movie, not just the Hollywood studios. He was way ahead of his time. Unlike the cliché when people say "I knew I wanted to be a filmmaker when I saw *Star Wars*," it didn't occur to me until *She's Gotta Have It*. Where this all leads to is my passions colliding—my love of photography and my love of literature. They marry together powerfully into that other medium which I love so much—the movies.

Film is alchemy. A movie is a collision of many arts. This includes photography, sound, music, architecture, fashion, arts

& crafts and makeup. Add the element of performance, and you have the ingredients for making a movie. Edit together this symphony of the arts and you can create a film. Yet, all of this starts on the blank screen or a blank piece of paper. This book intends to expand the writer's view of the medium itself. It is meant to make the reader think beyond the page and consider how a film works. Anyone who has made a movie knows that it doesn't end with the script. It is a fluid process—one that allows the filmmaker to react and change the final product to what he or she wanted, versus allowing it to be what it eventually arrives at. Things you think will work die, and things you think weren't working great end up soaring. Alchemy.

In the end, this book is meant to provoke thought about what it means to be a writer of moving pictures. Film is an entirely different beast than other artistic mediums, and thus one that needs specific, and special, consideration. So let us consider them—movies, and the writers who write them. Read on.

## EMPATHY

Empathy. This is one of the greatest concepts that any storyteller understands and is the essence of motion pictures. Master this concept and you will succeed as a writer and as a filmmaker. Film works best when it works in emotion and empathy. When someone says that they go to the movies to "escape," they are saying that they want to *experience* something. They want to experience joy and laughter (comedy), fear (horror), joy and sadness (drama), excitement (action adventure) and anxiety (mystery/thriller). There is not a better artistic medium that captures these emotions and it is the reason we love movies. This is something the screenwriter needs to understand. The combining of pictures and sound is powerful. It can be extremely moving and extremely visceral. What you need to do as a screenwriter is to aspire to those extremes. Understand the medium and wield it.

## KNOW THE MEDIUM – TAME THE BEAST

The movie is never as good as the book. This is the conventional wisdom of most audiences that enjoy both movies and books. These audiences are almost always disappointed in the film adaptation, which leads the screenwriter to ask, "Why is the movie never as good as the book?" The answer to this question reveals a lot about the differences between novels (and short stories) and film scripts. It is also an excellent place to start when thinking about writing a movie. Before we get into this, it is important to note that there are always exceptions to the rules.

And I will repeat this phrase many times over the course of this book. There are always exceptions. Is the book always better than the movie? No. Billy Wilder and Raymond Chandler improved James M. Cain's *Double Indemnity*. Cain had written the novel under pressure to deliver and didn't quite solve some issues with his plotting. Cain himself admitted that Wilder and Chandler had come up with great solutions to the problems he was having with the novel. There are also many who would say that Francis Ford Coppola and Mario Puzo improved what Puzo himself had written in the novel *The Godfather*. Again, there are always exceptions to the rule.

So what are the differences between writing a novel and writing a feature film? Why is the movie "never" as good as the novel? I like to think that writing for film is like putting on a pair of handcuffs. When you write for the movies you are handicapped by not having the ability to tell the audience what your characters think or feel. You have to *show* this. You cannot delve into the backstory of your characters. This is a form of digression and *film hates digression*. You need to be moving forward in your story or you are dead in the water. In film writing, we have dialogue, action, and editing. This is how we tell the story. What is your character doing? What are we learning from the dialogue? You cannot tell the audience what they are thinking unless you employ a voice-over. You cannot tell the audience exactly what they are feeling. You cannot break the scene to tell the audience that the feeling the character is having reminds them of how their father treated them as a kid. You could use a voice-over, or write a soliloquy or monologue, but these are not techniques that audiences expect in modern film. Woody Allen might break the scene and talk to the camera in *Annie Hall*, but this is one of those rare exceptions. Voice-over is the most used technique, but it has been derided over the years as being "lazy" writing. Voice-over was also a staple of old Hollywood, including the highly stylized track in Wilder and Chandler's classic *Double Indemnity*. In the modern day, film dislikes digression and voice-over is a last resort for a poorly written script. I will put the technique of voice-over off until later.

As an example of how a film is not like a novel or short story, we can look at Edgar Allen Poe's "The Cask of Amontillado." Poe is particularly interesting, as there have been many films made based on his writings and most have failed. Why? Most writers want to capture his macabre and psychological horror and translate it to film. This is aided by the fact that Poe's stories are in the public domain and free for any budding filmmaker to use.

Poe was one of the first writers of genre, and his texts have inspired many writers and readers of horror and mystery. Why have so many filmmakers failed at bringing these stories to the screen with any degree of success? Let us look at the opening of "The Cask of Amontillado" to see how much we can adapt for the screen.

*The thousand injuries of Fortunato I had borne as I best could, but when he ventured upon insult I vowed revenge. You, who so well know the nature of my soul,*

*will not suppose, however, that gave utterance to a
threat. At length I would be avenged; this was a point
definitely, settled—but the very definitiveness with
which it was resolved precluded the idea of risk. I must
not only punish but punish with impunity. A wrong is
unredressed when retribution overtakes its redresser. It
is equally unredressed when the avenger fails to make
himself felt as such to him who has done the wrong. It
must be understood that neither by word nor deed had
I given Fortunato cause to doubt my good will. I
continued, as was my wont, to smile in his face, and he
did not perceive that my smile now was at the thought
of his immolation.*

"Punish with impunity!" This is a great setup for a short story, but what is the film writer going to adapt? Poe has set up his story of revenge and punishment and the duplicity of the narrator. What do we see here? None of this is filmable. You might suggest a voice-over here but to what end and over what image? To think like a filmmaker, you need to shed that idea.

"You, who so well know the nature of my soul, will not suppose, however, that gave utterance to a threat."

The audience just sees a man on film, nothing more. What can we *show* the audience that makes them think "nature of his soul?" So far, nothing. Let us read on.

*He had a weak point —this Fortunato—although in
other regards he was a man to be respected and even*

*feared. He prided himself on his connoisseurship in wine. Few Italians have the true virtuoso spirit. For the most part their enthusiasm is adopted to suit the time and opportunity, to practise imposture upon the British and Austrian millionaires. In painting and gemmary, Fortunato, like his countrymen, was a quack, but in the matter of old wines he was sincere. In this respect I did not differ from him materially; —I was skilful in the Italian vintages myself, and bought largely whenever I could. It was about dusk, one evening during the supreme madness of the carnival season, that I encountered my friend. He accosted me with excessive warmth, for he had been drinking much. The man wore motley. He had on a tight-fitting parti-striped dress, and his head was surmounted by the conical cap and bells. I was so pleased to see him that I thought I should never have done wringing his hand. I said to him— "My dear Fortunato, you are luckily met. How remarkably well you are looking to-day. But I have received a pipe of what passes for Amontillado, and I have my doubts."*

Now let's put this into screenplay format.

```
EXT. CARNIVALE - NIGHT

FORTUNATO, wearing a tight-fitting parti-
striped dress and conical cap and bells,
approaches Montresor. Fortunato is not sure
on his feet as he's had too much to drink.
```

<pre>
Montresor greets him with a firm handshake
and a large smile.

                    MONTRESOR

My dear Fortunato, you are luckily met. How
remarkably well you are looking today. But I
have received a pipe of what passes for
Amontillado, and I have my doubts.
</pre>

There is a lot of information in Poe's story as written, but what is useful for the film writer? The idea of revenge has no context on screen. If we start to build a scene, we will see two men meeting and there can be a little bit of dialogue representing some niceties but nothing else. How do we know about Fortunato's "connoisseurship of wine?" What is said in the film scene that tells the audience what Poe has already told us so easily in the story? Do we know its Carnival season? Does it matter? Showing this might cost the production a lot of money. The audience has no idea of the narrator's fondness of wine and we have no idea that Fortunato has a weakness, in that, he needs to be respected and feared. An audience in a theater has not learned anything, even though the written story has given us many details. You might ask, why not create a narrator like the book? To this I say, you are missing the entire point. Let us move on.

What happens next is that Montresor lures Fortunato to the damp catacombs towards the Cask of Amontillado. He has sent his staff home for the night, and Montresor plays with his victim by giving him ample opportunity to go back; but Fortunato wants to drink the rare Sherry in the cask. Eventually, when they get to the end of their journey, in what Poe describes as a niche,

Montresor binds Fortunato to the wall with chains. He gets to work quickly, and with trowel and brick, he walls Fortunato in. We find out at the end of the story that half a century later, no one has ever discovered the remains of Fortunato.

There is a lot of appeal in Poe's work for a filmmaker. His story drips with dread and atmosphere. His description of the catacombs leads the visual imagination into places that film loves—moody lighting, texture and shadow. There is a high sense of drama from the life and death struggle of Fortunato and the sinister plan by Montresor. The problem is that fundamentally, it is not a filmic story, although it feels like it should be. Why? The answer lies in the fact that most of this story is dependent on Montresor, who is the narrator of the story. This is his revenge. What is he avenging? Even the story itself is quite slight on this. As we read earlier, he justifies his revenge based on Fortunato's "insult." For this his murder will be done as punishment and punishment with impunity.

In adapting this to a more filmic narrative, what does the audience need to know, and how do they get this information? Remember, we aren't using the voice-over as a crutch (it wouldn't make the film any better if you were to use it). The audience needs to understand the nature of Fortunato's "insult." This is the question of *why* the story is taking place. Most likely, this would have to be done with dialogue. You might write the dialogue for Montresor while he is busy building the wall of bricks. This is the murderer's time for confession, but this takes on a James Bond villain technique (or what *The Incredibles* referred satirically to as *monologuing*).

The main problem with "The Cask of Amontillado" is that it is an interior story where very little happens. It is in the mind of Montresor, and our experience with the story is through that point of view. Despite a weak reason for revenge, the story has an element of horror and darkness that draws us in. Poe's use of the catacombs and their vivid description lights our imagination. Unfortunately, this does not translate well to film. Film is not an *interior* medium—it is an *external* medium. This means that we are more involved in a story when the characters are doing something that reveals character. In this story, we see Montresor lure Fortunato to the catacombs, and he effectively buries him alive. So what? Who does the audience engage with? Do we want Montresor to succeed in his revenge? We don't even know what Fortunato has done, and an "insult" doesn't really justify this act of madness. Poe's story works because of the interior voice of Montresor and the reader's own imagination. In film, we build the sets and watch the action unfold, and there is little need for imagination. For this story to work on film, we would have to create a story outside of this story. We would have to invent the incident where Montresor is slighted so the audience can relate to the story and to Montresor's point of view. We would start to ask what Montresor wants from Fortunato that he has been denied, and we would ask the same of Fortunato. What does Fortunato want from Montresor? What would cause such a grave insult? The idea here is that we want to relate to these characters in the world of film so that we care about the outcome. What if the audience knew that Fortunato had plans to give Montresor what he wanted and is bricked up before the information gets out? The murder then becomes tragic. And you will say that I am messing with Poe's story too much. And I will say that the film will not be as good as the book. Poe's story is not a film story.

Even the scene where Fortunato is bound and bricked up needs careful consideration. The idea of being bricked in and left to die in the dark is horrific for the reader. What you need to consider as a filmmaker is how this will take place in time. How will it play? We might be intrigued when Fortunato is bound and curious as to what Montresor has in store for him. Yet, laying bricks is not an exciting thing to watch. He might as well grab a paintbrush and paint the place too. It works in the novel because Poe can just say it and time is not a factor for the reader. It occurs in their imagination. In film it needs to play. Adding a big dissolve right after Montresor lays the first brick will kill any tension the scene has. Film has great tools to compress time (editing and transitions), but to do this in the climax of your story seems ludicrous. It becomes a big problem.

How do you sustain the tension for the audience? How do you sustain the dread and horror?

To bring Poe's story to life on film, the writer would have to do a lot of inventing, and this is where the fan of the book will say the film isn't as good as the book. Often the reader fails to understand why his or her favorite characters or incidents were cut out of the movie, and there is a great amount of disappointment because the film cannot contain the contents of the book. There is also an entirely different pace and narrative drive with books and movies.

This brings us to one of the fundamental things that writers should ask themselves: Is my idea a good "film" idea? Having taught writing for years, I have found that many of my students want to write films but often submit ideas that are better suited for the theater. They write scenes that are verbal exchanges between characters in singular locations. If it works better, write it as a play. I will tell you this—you will have a much better chance of someone seeing your work if you write it as a play. Film is an expensive and logistically difficult medium and it is hard to get anything made and even harder to get it seen.

A prime example of an idea that is well suited for film is Alfred Hitchcock's *Rear Window,* based on Cornell Woolrich's short story, "It Had to be Murder." It is the story of a voyeur who thinks he has witnessed a murder based on the unexplained circumstances he has seen in an apartment across the courtyard. Just as Hal Jeffries is the witness in the book, the audience becomes a witness in the film (with Jeffries played by Jimmy Stewart). Even though this story was meant to be short fiction, it begged for a film treatment as the nature of the story was of the protagonist *watching,* an ideal concept for a movie. What makes this material outstanding is that it centers on a character who comes to conclusions about an event based on what he *sees.* He watches the actions of his neighbor across the courtyard, and he comes to conclusions based on what he has seen. It is a perfect story for film. Just as Jeffries sees the actions of his neighbor, we see them also. We can judge Jeffries based on what we have seen because we, as the audience, are participants in the experience of the protagonist. This is a purely cinematic idea and one that Hitchcock seized on in making this film.

It is very interesting to see *Rear Window* develop from the short story to Hitchcock's film, adapted superbly by John Michael Hayes. The short story is quite simple and sparse, and Hayes and Hitchcock had to invent a great deal of story to fill in the two-hour running time. The short story basically has three characters: Jeffries, his houseman Sam, and the detective Boyne.

Thorwald is the object of Jeffries suspicion. In the adaptation Hayes and Hitchcock created, Lisa Fremont (Grace Kelly) is a model and the love interest for Jeffries. Jeffries, a freewheeling adventurer and professional photographer, resists a committed relationship for fear that it might change his high-octane lifestyle. Hays and Hitchcock change the fairly straight character of the houseman Sam to a wise-cracking Stella (Thelma Ritter). They also flesh out the story with small silent stories of the neighbors across the courtyard. In addition, Hayes and Hitchcock invent "Miss Lonelyhearts," the frustrated Songwriter, "Miss Torso," and they expand on the newlyweds. For the most part, the main thrust of the short story provides the blueprint for the structure of the film. Jeffries notices that Thorwald's wife is no longer with him, and he begins to believe that Thorwald has murdered her in the apartment, dismembered her body, and buried her somewhere.

What makes *Rear Window* so cinematic and a great example of visual story telling is that we see what Jeffries sees. We never change this perspective. We see what he sees and we must come to the conclusion that his imagination has gone into overdrive, or that Thorwald has indeed murdered his wife. We experience the film through Jeffries, and this is one of the great concepts of filmmaking.

## *THE EMPIRE STRIKES BACK* VERSUS *ATTACK OF THE CLONES*

To try to illuminate the point further, we can compare the two middle films in the *Star Wars* trilogies. Both of these films start out with a bang. The first act of *The Empire Strikes Back* starts with the Rebels being discovered on the ice planet Hoth. Luke learns of the Jedi Master Yoda, and the Rebels flee when Vader arrives and a battle ensues. The first act of *Attack of the Clones* features an attempted assassination of Senator Padmé Amidala. She is put under the protection of Obiwan and Anakin, and upon the second attempt on her life, a large scale hunt ensues with the two Jedis attempting to capture the assassin. The assassin is killed by a poison dart sent from a second assassin before they can identify who is behind the plot to kill the Senator.

This is where the two films diverge. In *Empire*, Luke escapes and makes his way to find Yoda in order to complete his training as a Jedi. This is a very active idea and the audience has to go on this journey with him. In the subplot of *Empire*, Han, Leia, Chewbacca, and the Droids are under heavy pursuit by Imperial Starships. Their hyperdrive is broken and they can't jump to light speed to get away.

In *Attack of the Clones*, Obiwan discovers the source of the poison from the dart, and he is sent to the planet Kamino to investigate. Again, Obiwan is active, and there is a mystery to be solved. In the subplot, Anakin is sent to Naboo to protect the Senator, who is going to be hidden away from further attempts on her life. Now, this seems to be an active goal, but it turns out that nothing actually happens. There is no danger or tension in these scenes, and they seem to be designed to be "conversations" that would lead to the development of the love story. This is where the story halts and the audience gets restless.

In *The Empire Strikes Back*, Han and Leia's love story is developed while they are *doing* something. Little moments are drawn out while they try to fix the hyperdrive. It happens while they duck and dodge their Imperial pursuers. There is momentum and tension in the story, and during this Han and Leia learn that they are attracted to each other, and this culminates in the third act where love is professed. This is a very cinematic approach. We learn about characters as they *do* things and react to the pressures of the conflict. Compare this to the development of the love story in *Attack of the Clones*. Everything that happens, happens though dialogue. At one point, they are discussing politics during a picnic and Anakin hints at his dislike of democracy and his interest in an autocratic rule. In literature, this is called "foreshadowing," but in this film, there is no need for it. What they need to do is show us. What does Anakin *do* that suggests he doesn't like democracy? Does he shut down all discussion and make everyone go with his ideas? Since nothing actually happens on Naboo, the answer is no. It is all tell and no show.

This is what "visual" story telling means. It isn't symbolism; it's about trying to express your story through the actions of your characters. If you were to remove the dialogue, would the audience get a sense of what is going on? If the answer is yes, then your film is working as a film.

If the answer is no, then you might be writing a radio play.

## THE CLEAN LINE OF ACTION – KEEP IT SIMPLE

One of Billy Wilder's rules is to create a "clean line of action" for your character. That is to say, what is his or her overall goal in the story? This is important for the audience; they want to know where the story is going, and your job is to bring them along, and then surprise them. The writer raises the expectation of the audience then breaks that expectation and surprises them with unexpected turns. As Alexander Mackendrick said, "What is happening now isn't as interesting as what will happen next." The clean line of action tells the audience where the story is going, but it doesn't give away how your character will get there.

Here are some examples of the clean line of action.

*Star Wars*: Save the princess

*Lord of the Rings*: Throw the ring into the mountain

*The Bourne Identity*: Find out 'who I am'

*Saving Private Ryan*: Save Private Ryan

*The Godfather*: Protect the family

*The Dark Knight*: Stop the Joker

*Back to the Future*: Get back to the future

*Rear Window*: Find out what happened to the absent wife

*12 Angry Men*: Come to a verdict

*The Seven Samurai*: Protect the village

*Raiders of the Lost Ark*: Recover the Ark and keep it out of the hands of the Nazis

*Se7en*: Find the serial killer before he kills again

*Silence of the Lambs*: Find Buffalo Bill before he kills the governor's daughter

*The Terminator*: Protect Sarah Connor from the Terminator

*Terminator 2*: Protect John Connor from the Terminator.

*Rocky*: Win the title fight

*Die Hard*: Stop the terrorists

*The Fugitive*: Find the real killer and prove innocence

*The Hangover*: Find the groom

*Superbad*: Get the booze to the party

*The Exorcist*: Exorcise the demon

*Apocalypse Now*: Terminate Kurtz (with extreme prejudice).

There is a fear for some writers that a simple line of action might compromise their idea and that the audience will not be interested. It is the writer's job to surprise the audience and break their expectations along the way. We know that Luke is going to leave Tatooine to save Princess Leia, but we have no idea how he is going to do this and neither does he. The goal need not be complicated. But accomplishing the goal should be.

Not every film adheres to this rule, but the spirit of the rules should be in the writer's mind. What does the audience know? Do they have a sense of where the story is going? Will they be interested in what happens next if they have no idea where the scene or scenes are leading?

Most people, including some industry folk, think that the writer's job is dialogue. They fail to understand that the writer creates the story and dialogue is just a component of that story. I once sat in story meetings with a producer who asked if we could skip over reading the action and just read the dialogue. It was a ridiculous request, and when we read only the dialogue, no one knew what the hell was going on. You did not know what the characters were *doing* as the dialogue was reacting to what was happening. To please this producer, I ended up ad-libbing what was going on in the action, otherwise he would have had no idea what was *happening*.

So what is a story? Simply put, a story consists of a character (protagonist) with a goal he or she seeks to achieve. What stands in his or her way? What are the opposing forces? Think of *Lord of the Rings*. What is the goal of the protagonist Frodo? Throw the ring in the fire. It is a simple and clean line of action, but it is not that simple for little Frodo as there are strong forces that also want the ring (opposing goals). What about Jason Bourne?

His goal is to find out his real identity. But that is not easy when the C.I.A.'s opposing goal is to terminate him.

*Star Wars?* Luke's goal is to save the Princess from the evil and powerful Empire. The opposing goal is Vader and Tarkin's need to find the secret rebel base in order to quash the rebellion. In *Rear Window*, Jeffries' goal is to find out what happened to his neighbor's wife. In *The Third Man*, Martins wants to expose his friend Harry Lime's death as a homicide and not an accident. Even in a complex film like *Citizen Kane* there is a simple goal —to discover who Kane really was as a man. Welles's use of a fractured structure makes it seem more complicated than it is. In all of these films, you can go beat-by-beat and look at what it is that is stopping the protagonists from achieving their goals.

You can break these films down into smaller goals (scenes) that lead to the overall goal. In *Lord of the Rings*, for example, Frodo is told to take the ring and meet Gandalf at the Prancing Pony Inn. Gandalf's goal is to meet Frodo after meeting with Saruman, a wizard of great power.

Gandalf's goal is thwarted when he is imprisoned by Saruman, who is in the service of the "Dark Lord" Sauron. Little Frodo's goal is to reach the Inn, a goal that is in conflict with the Horsemen who have been dispatched to the Shire to kill him and retrieve the ring. Frodo and his friends barely escape the riders and achieve the goal of getting to the Inn only to face a new challenge: Gandalf is not there. A new goal must be created to move along to the overall goal of the story: throw the ring into Mount Doom to defeat Sauron. This is how the story unfolds, and the writer hopes that each step of the way provides the audience with tension and anticipation.

"When is something going to happen"? This is what the audience says when a story is not set up properly. The writer may have introduced some characters and has them all talking about things, but the audience only becomes interested when they have an idea where the story is going to lead. This is where the term "the inciting incident" comes in. This is the answer to "When is something going to happen?" And it tells us where the story might lead us.

In Joel and Ethan Coen's film *No Country for Old Men*, the inciting incident is the discovery of the case full of cash by Llewelyn Moss. Keep in mind that the "inciting incident" isn't when Moss *discovers* the cash but when he decides to *take* it. The story only moves forward when something happens. If he leaves the money and walks away, the credits will roll. So what is stopping him from keeping the money and living happily ever after? The opposing goals of those who want the money back, one of whom is cinema's greatest villains, Chigurh.

*No Country for Old Men* is an interesting film for another reason. Watching the film, you get a sense that Llewelyn is the protagonist. After all, he seems to have a strong goal and we want to see him succeed. Yet, he is killed in the third act of the film in an off-screen incident. This causes a lot of discomfort for the audience as the protagonist is rarely killed off, especially when we don't even get to witness it. Hitchcock did this in *Psycho* in a much more extreme way. Marion Crane is murdered at the end of the first act, leaving the audience emotionally displaced and confused. So who is the protagonist in *No Country for Old Men?* It seems that the Sheriff, Ed Bell, played by Tommy Lee Jones, is our reluctant protagonist. His goal is to stop Chigurh and solve the crime. This is one of those wonderful films that breaks the rules for a reason. Bell opens the film with narration.

> *"The crime you see now, it's hard to even take its measure. It's not that I'm afraid of it. I always knew you had to be willing to die to even do this job. But, I don't want to push my chips forward and go out and meet something I don't understand. A man would have to put his soul at hazard. He'd have to say, "O.K., I'll be part of this world."*

At the beginning of the film, Sheriff Bell states his reluctance to face the likes of Chigurh. He doesn't want to be a part of the world of the film, but he has a job and a duty to do just that. The film ends in a whimper, with a retired Bell reciting a dream he had about his father carrying a torch forward. The end of the film deals more with theme than plot and seems more like an epilogue. I will talk later about personal films versus commercial films, and how elements of story are open to rule-breaking for loftier ambitions. It is also worth pointing out that *No Country* is from the imagination of Cormac McCarthy and is an adaptation of his novel. Screenwriters tend to take a lot of liberties with adaptations, for the purposes outlined earlier, and the Coens could have straightened out all of the lines, but they chose stay close to the source material.

In basic story structure, you have a protagonist and an antagonist. Here you have goals and opposing goals. Often people think of this relationship as a hero and a villain. This works for comic book movies and action films, but in drama, the antagonist doesn't have to be a "villain." Take Jim Taylor and Alexander Payne's wonderful film *Sideways*, adapted from Rex Pickett's novel. In the story, Miles (Paul Giamatti) wants to take his college friend out for a week of golf and winery tours before his friend gets married. This seems to be a simple goal. His friend Jack, played to perfection by Thomas Haden Church, has other ideas. He wants to use this week to sow his wild oats one last time before his marriage. The problem is that Miles has gone through a rough divorce and just wants to spend his time sipping wine, eating well, and knocking some balls around. Jack, the "antagonist," wants Miles to let go and have fun, but Miles isn't ready; he is obsessing about his ex-wife (who is coming to the wedding with her new man). Jack is the most active character, creating situations that force Miles to act and react. The film moves along with a great balance of humor and drama as both men seek to achieve their goals.

In Robert Zemeckis' film *Castaway*, nature becomes the antagonist to the main character's goal of survival and his need to get off the island. *Castaway* is an interesting film because for much of the movie there is very little dialogue. When the film was released, audiences wondered how a film with very little dialogue could be interesting. The answer is—you guessed it—*goals*. Once stranded on the island, Chuck (Tom Hanks) has some life-and-death needs. He needs fresh water to survive, and when you are on an island in the middle of a salt water ocean, fresh water can be extremely difficult to come by. Of course, the answer is coconuts; the island is full of them. But how do you break into a coconut? This becomes one of the first goals of the protagonist, and the audience wants to see him achieve it. He needs food. He also needs to see if there are any other inhabitants on the island. He needs to build a fire and a raft to escape. And so on, and so forth. All along the way, the audience wants to see him succeed because, well, he is Tom Hanks and we like him. Our empathy takes us through the story.

A *story* is the story of a character's journey to get what he or she needs. The "stakes" are what will be lost if that character doesn't get it, and this is what makes the story fly.

The clean line of action helps propel the story forward. The audience empathizes with the protagonist and sits on the edge of their seats, hoping the protagonist will get what it is that he or she seeks. If the audience is uncertain where the story is going, they will get restless and start to tune out. Audiences love to "play along" and are delighted when something they thought was going to happen doesn't happen and something new comes along. Build expectation, and then break it.

## YES, DIALOGUE IS IMPORTANT, BUT NOT THAT IMPORTANT

Dialogue is an important tool, but it isn't as important as you think. I get a lot of hostility when I talk about this, as people are fixated on dialogue as the driving mechanism of the story. It is not. Dialogue serves two purposes in a film story. The first is information or, as we refer to it in the industry, *exposition* (information is exposed). The second function is to reveal character. What someone says, and how they say it, reveals much about that character.

In terms of exposition, some things are hard to show. Think of the films *Inception* and *The Matrix*. Both films have a lot of action, but both films require the audience to learn a lot about the world they are in. The films have to teach the characters and the audience about the rules of those worlds in order for the story to make sense. In *The Matrix*, we enter the world from the point of view of the protagonist, Neo, and we learn, as he does, about the universe of the film. In *Inception*, Ariadne is our way into the world of the film. She is taught, as we in the audience are too, how the dream world works. Without these "lessons," we would be lost. This is classic exposition. *The Matrix* handles this better, as Neo (Reeves) is the protagonist, and we follow him down the rabbit hole. "Inception" is a bit clumsier because we need to ask ourselves if Ariadne (Page) is a strong character with her own goals. Her place in the story seems to be for the benefit of the audience and not herself. She is not the protagonist. What is her need in the story? What happens if she doesn't take the job of the architect? What is at stake for her if she says no to the journey?

The use of exposition is required in most films and is best used when the characters in your story need to know the information.

Many young screenwriters feel they need to provide the entire context for the story right away. A common and terrible example of this is two characters each telling the other something that he or she already knows. The audience feels like a little play has been staged just for them to learn something. These scenes tend to have no dramatic tension, as the intention is to provide the audience with information.

Young screenwriters aren't the only ones making this mistake. I pointed out earlier that *Rear Window*, a cinematic classic by a master, has a very poor scene of exposition in the first act. Jeff (Stewart) is visited by Stella (Ritter), a nurse provided by insurance to look after him while still in his leg cast. Stella begins to give Jeff a massage, and the conversation spins on about Jeff and his girlfriend Lisa's incompatible lifestyles. The scene drags on for a bit and is only saved by Ritter's spirited performance and some sharp banter that is trying to hide the sheer amount of exposition going on. The question is whether this information could have been allowed to come out naturally, as it does when Lisa shows up? Do we need to have all this explanation in a scene that has no drama? Having said that, there is a structural problem for Hitchcock and Hayes regarding Stella. If they do skip this scene of exposition, she wouldn't show up in the film until much later, and they don't want to be introducing major new characters a half hour or more into the film. The scene with Jeff allows the audience to meet her and get to know her, so that when she returns after Jeff suspects the neighbor of murder, she is already established. Remember that film does not like digression, so introducing Stella after the inciting incident becomes problematic because you would be spending your time explaining who she is and what she is doing there. The audience isn't interested at that point—they want to know about the potential of "murder." So creating this little scene of exposition is useful for the audience in terms of knowing Jeff and his situation, and it solves the problem of introducing Stella to the audience. That this scene comes very early in the film is helpful, so if the audience is getting a little restless, Hitchcock makes them forget about it once the suspense and mystery get started.

*Rear Window* remains a classic, despite this clunky scene, and it is a perfect example of terrific point-of-view filmmaking. We see what Jeff sees, and we come to conclusions based on our own experience of the film. What is happening to him is happening to us. There are also little silent films within the film as we observe the neighbors and see their stories unfold *without dialogue.*

## EXAMPLES OF GREAT DIALOGUE

*"Were going to need a bigger boat."*

*"Who are those guys?"*

*"Leave the gun. Take the cannoli."*

*"Is it safe?"*

*"Frankly My Dear, I don't give a damn."*

*"I coulda been a contender."*

*"Take your stinkin' paws off me, you damn dirty ape."*

*"I'll be back."*

*"You talkin' to me?"*

*"I – drink – your – milkshake! I drink it up!"*

*"I'm going to make him an offer he can't refuse."*

*"Here's looking at you, kid."*

*"May the Force be with you."*

*"Show me the money!"*

*"I see dead people."*

*"Soylent Green is people!"*

*"So nice to see you."*

*"Hasta la vista, baby."*

*"Nobody puts Baby in a corner."*

*"I'm the king of the world!"*

These are all memorable lines of dialogue from classic films. After you have seen one of these films, you can't help but smile when you hear it quoted. To someone who has not seen these films, the words are meaningless. Great dialogue is all in the context in which the words are uttered. Without the audience seeing the massive shark swim past the boat in *Jaws*, "We're going to need a bigger boat" doesn't mean anything. What is *happening* in the story is the thing that makes it special.

Tarantino's "Royal with cheese" bit in *Pulp Fiction* works wonderfully, as it is placed between a robbery and a hit. He also gives the dialogue to two hit men who are not like many hit men in film history. The audience tends to think of the hit man as the lonely recluse, as in Besson's *Leon: The Professional.* The dialogue is comedic, but nothing more inspiring than any good comic could come up with. Placed in terms of context and character, the dialogue comes alive. (It also helps that Sam Jackson is saying the lines.)

In *No Country for Old Men*, Chigurh stops for gasoline and there is a riveting scene of dialogue between him and the proprietor. Chigurh offers a coin toss and asks him, "What's the most you've ever lost on a coin toss?" The man is confused and terrified because Chigurh is menacing and confrontational. The scene drips with tension, and on the surface, it feels like it is being driven by dialogue. However, in context of the story, we've just witnessed Chigurh kill a cop and murder another man for his car. With that knowledge, the scene carries the weight of those violent acts. We know what Chigurh is about and we know that the poor old innocent proprietor is about to be dispatched with the same amount of callous disregard for human life as the other two. We fear for him, and we empathize with him. The dialogue in the scene is well written and performed to perfection. However, if you put this scene first in the movie, before we see Chigurh kill, it would carry far less tension. Context is everything. Story is everything.

Great dialogue and witty exchanges are wonderful things. It adds icing on the cake of a well-filmed story. It reveals character and deepens the themes of the story, and it is important. Just not as important as everyone thinks.

In 1970, *M*A*S*H* was released, and as legend has it, very little of Ring Larder Jr.'s dialogue was used. According to many, the film was mostly ad-libbed, and it isn't surprising, considering director Robert Altman's unusual style and approach to film-making. In an ironic twist, Lardner won the academy award for the screenplay, despite having "written" very little of it. Or so the story goes. I go back to my original point here, *M*A*S*H* is a story. It is a wonderfully funny collection of episodic vignettes, and this structure and the ideas within the story come from the writer. Ad-libbing dialogue is not the hard work. The hard work is creating those scenes and tying them together into a cohesive story. The hard work is creating the drama. The characters are created, the story is provided, and then you can ad-lib all you want. It is much harder to ad-lib story. The great Larry David employed this in his cult show *Curb Your Enthusiasm*. David writes out all of the story outlines and then improvises the dialogue with his brilliant improvisational troop of actors. David knows that they can come up with some good banter within the scenes, but he doesn't improvise story. The story is thought out and well-constructed in advance. This allows the actors to know where they need to go in the scene, and they can play with it as they move to the next beat of story.

It is maddening when ad-libbed dialogue impresses people. The writer ad-libs the dialogue all the time.

## WRITE WHAT YOU KNOW – FIND OUT WHAT YOU DON'T KNOW

The hardest part of writing a story is coming up with a great idea or character. There are many books out there that will try to make the act of writing seem complicated. You will see all sorts of diagrams and hear talk about the "hero's journey" and fixed story beats. The truth is that a character has a goal and he or she struggles to achieve it. The hard part is coming up with that great character and his or her antagonist. The problem is not in how to write a story but how to solve the creative problem of dreaming one up.

Woody Allen has been criticized a lot over the latter part of his career. I remember when *Bullets Over Broadway* came out, one reviewer actually said, "It's good but it's no *Annie Hall*." Of course it's no *Annie Hall*! *Annie Hall* is one of Allen's greatest films and very much deserving of its Academy Award for best film of that year (beating out *Star Wars*). The point to be made here is that Woody Allen has made over forty original feature films. He wrote these films from a blank page on a piece of paper. This is on top of his original plays and works of prose. What artist is going to be able to produce an *Annie Hall* forty times over? Especially when the creative well is what is inside you. Even William Shakespeare has "lesser works."

There are other wonderful writing filmmakers, like Coppola, Kurosawa, Kubrick, and Spielberg, but their work includes a good deal of adaptations from books or other mediums. Original work is hard to do and it is hard to sell. And for Woody Allen to produce the volume of work he has, it is no wonder that he misses the mark sometimes. It is more important to be working than to be creating perfection.

Where do we get our stories? The great Canadian writer Mordecai Richler once said if you want to be a writer, become a shoe salesman first. This was his way of saying "write what you know."

Most aspiring writers have heard this stated. Write what you know. If you want to be writer, experience something in life to write about. This is not to say that imagination isn't an immense part of the equation because it is. As human beings, we have the gift of empathy and the ability to imagine ourselves outside of our own consciousness and bodies. The mouse, as far as science knows, doesn't look at the elephant and think to itself, "It must be awesome to be so big." Writing what you know adds truth to the imagination, and that is what makes for a great story. You don't have to go any further than David Simon's lauded series *The Wire* to see this. David Simon is a terrific storyteller and journalist. What made *The Wire* so special for audiences was that it felt real. It felt real because there are so many unique details in the stories that any writer of "imagination" wouldn't have put in. The characters have a ring of truth because they are facsimiles of real characters that Simon and his partner Ed Burns have known. The show went beyond the normal cops and robbers procedurals and told the stories with truth and imagination. David Simon spent a year with homicide detectives in Baltimore and wrote the book *Homicide: A Year on the Killing Streets.* His writing partner, Ed Burns, is a former cop and teacher. These guys knew what they were talking about, and they knew all of the details and specifics of that world. This makes it rich because they wrote what they knew and what they knew was truth.

When Paramount Studio needed to make a film adaptation of Mario Puzo's best-selling novel *The Godfather,* they decided to go with a director of Italian-American heritage. Coppola and Puzo turned out to be a great pair, and Coppola brought his own sensibility and experiences to the adaptation. Of note was the big wedding celebration at the beginning of the film. It doesn't feel staged, and it is full of specific details that make it special. Coppola wrote down little vignettes in his notebook that came from his own memories of Italian weddings. He wrote things like:

"Kids in little suits 'sliding around the sandwich man'."

"Throwing the Sandwiches."

"Fat, older man dancing with a ten year old girl in a confirmation dress. Her little shoes on his big ones."

All of these personal, specific details add to the feeling of truth and honesty.

The ironic thing here is that Puzo wrote his novel out of research and imagination (he had no experience with the mafia).

And the mafia wasn't something that Coppola knew at all, but he did know what it was like to grow up in an Italian American family. A lot of what is memorable about *The Godfather* is that it doesn't feel like a normal genre film. It feels personal.

"Take the cannoli, leave the gun." This is a famous line from the film. The idea of the cannoli came from Coppola's own experience with an aunt who used to say, "Don't forget the cannoli." He brings this into a scene of murder, and it gives it a specific richness of culture and memory. It adds what he knows about family, and the importance of family is to not forget the cannoli.

James Cameron's megahit, *Titanic*, was also a product of great research and imagination. It also came out of obsession. We do know that Cameron wasn't on the Titanic, but he went out of his way to find those wonderful little details that take a film to the next level. He used the film as an excuse to dive down to the sunken Titanic and explore it. The film is the work of obsession and knowledge mixed with a good degree of imagination. What Cameron knows is the entire story of the Titanic, as well as the science that allowed the vessel to sink to the bottom of the sea. He is concerned with the lower classes left to die and the aristocrats who lived. James Cameron fashions his tragic story out of research and knowledge with a good degree of imagination and craftsmanship.

Passion matters.

One big problem with many amateur screenplays is that the writers write from a place of bullshit. They write a cop story without any knowledge of what a real cop does. They write a war story with no knowledge of war. I find that most amateur scripts are references to movies and not to life. For the audience, this becomes derivative, where the film becomes cliché, vague, and uninteresting.

When you don't know what you're talking about, find out. Imagination is great, but truth comes from experience and knowledge (research).

Write what you know and find out what you don't know. The script will only get better when it is more defined, specific, and original. I could not have written a good divorce drama before I got divorced. I know that now that I have been through the experience. All of what *I thought* would be important wasn't that important. As a point of detail, I knew my marriage had ended when my wife bought me a birthday present and card. The card was signed from our cat. Only the cat. You can't make that stuff up. After the birth of my twin daughters, I realized that if someone had asked me to write a story about new parents, I would have got it totally wrong. I had no idea what it was like to be a parent, and it would have all been a pack of lies.

The devil is in the details, and it shows when you don't know any of the details. The films that are born out of ignorance are the ones that seem terribly contrived and cliché. They are vague, at best.

# THEME WILL GUIDE YOU

There are all sorts of theories about where to start when writing a new screenplay. Often there is a treatment, which is a short telling of the overall plot and story. There is also an outline where the writer expands on the treatment and outlines more details of subplot. It may also contain dialogue. I have seen outlines that stretch out over sixty pages long. Do you need to write an outline or treatment? Absolutely not—unless someone is paying you to do so. I have read many dogmatic approaches on how to start writing, but it is mostly just personal preference. Whatever works for you. That is the proper answer. Do you need an ending to start writing? Absolutely not. If your character has a goal you will eventually figure it out. I prefer not to work with an ending, as I find that if you have a determined ending you start to create false moments in trying to get to that ending. I much prefer working from a premise and theme and see where the story leads. I usually have an idea of where I am going, but I don't try to work it out in advance. As the Coen brothers point out, if *they* don't know how the film is going to end while writing it, how will *the audience* figure it out? This works for me but doesn't work for others. Some people are adamant that you need to have an ending and you need to create an outline. To them I say that *they* need to have an ending, but *you* can do what works for you. If an outline works for you, write an outline. If it doesn't, write the script. The most important thing is that your character has a goal and a need to fulfill that goal.

Remember to always let *theme* guide you while writing a story. What is your story about? What question are you raising? What question are you trying to answer? A great example of this is Krzysztof Kieslowski and his writing partner Krzysztof Piesiewicz. The two Polish writers collaborated on *The Dekalog* and *Three Colors: Red, White and Blue*. All of these films were created out of theme.

Stanley Kubrick wrote this forward to the printed screenplays of *The Dekalog*.

> *"I am always reluctant to single out some particular feature of the work of a major filmmaker because it tends inevitably to simplify and reduce the work. But in this book of screenplays by Krzysztof Kieslowski and his co-author, Krzysztof Piesiewicz, it should not be out of place to observe that they have the very rare ability to dramatize their ideas rather than just talking about them. By making their points through the dramatic action of the story they gain the added power of allowing the audience to discover what's really going on rather than being told. They do this with such dazzling skill, you never see the ideas coming and don't realize until much later how profoundly they have reached your heart." – Stanley Kubrick*

In *The Dekalog*, Kieslowski and Piesiewicz took on the *Bible* and created ten one-hour films based on each of the Ten Commandments. Each story was created with a thematic question and a moral conundrum derived from each commandment. What is particularly great about their films is life is seldom as simple or as black-and-white as the commandments suggest. Each film creates a moral ambiguity that challenges the idea of the certainty of the moral value. Each story is approached from the thematic point of view. The plot and drama serve to question the moral statement in each commandment. Kubrick is also praising the filmmakers' ability to do this through visual story-telling.

In the *Three Colors* trilogy, Kieslowski and Piesiewicz tackle the three colors of the French flag and what they represent: fraternity, equality and liberty. Each film uses the theme as the compass for the telling of the story. On one level, they are trying to tell a coherent story with characters who have clear goals and a desire to achieve those goals. On another level, the filmmakers are trying to answer the questions of the theme. What do these things mean? Liberty is freedom. What does freedom mean? Physical or psychological?

The most cinematic of these three films is *Blue* starring Juliette Binoche. Kieslowski and Piesiewicz create a story around the theme of liberty. The theme is the thing that creates the story. What is brilliant about these filmmakers/writers is that they don't approach this idea in a big Hollywood way; instead, they create a small, nuanced cinematic drama with the idea of *liberty* at heart. Julie (Binoche) is in a car accident in which she loses her daughter and husband. We discover that her husband was a famous music composer working on a very important piece for "the reunification of Europe." It remains unfinished after his death. Slowly we start to discover that Julie may have been the composer of this work, but in keeping with the idea of liberty, Julie has given up everything she owns and has decided to start a new life. She seeks liberty from her past, her daughter's death, her music, and most of all, herself. It is a brilliant film and one born out of theme and meaning. How can one find liberty from oneself? It is an impossible endeavor. As Ralph Waldo Emerson once said, "My giant goes with me wherever I go." This is the thing that drives the film's narrative.

There is a great moment in *Hearts of Darkness: A Filmmakers Apocalypse*, the documentary of the making of *Apocalypse Now*, where Coppola says he intended to make an exciting action movie from the script written by John Milius, but he kept running into the questions that the story was asking. The film is about every human's capacity for cruelty and evil. It is about lies and contradictions. Kurtz has gone mad, but in a way, he is the only pure character in the film. He was asked to wage war and that is what he has done; he wages war without morality, as war is itself immoral. As Willard says in the beginning of the film, "Charging a man with murder in this place was like handing out speeding tickets in the Indy 500." The dialogue is a statement of theme and it is brought through the thread of the narrative. Later in the film, Willard and his men open fire on a river boat and massacre the boat's passengers. One woman barely survives, and the soldiers want to take her to a hospital. Willard shoots her in the head.

*"It's a way we had over here for living with ourselves. We cut 'em in half with a machine gun and give 'em a Band-Aid. It was a lie. And the more I saw them, the more I hated lies." – Willard in Apocalypse Now*

The end of *Apocalypse Now* is famous, as Coppola abandoned Milius's ending because it didn't do anything to answer the themes of the film. Milius had Willard and Kurtz fighting together in a big epic battle. Coppola realized that this didn't work with the theme. What is the meaning of this action? What does it say about lies and contradictions and the darkness within us? When Brando showed up to play Kurtz, Coppola didn't have his ending yet, and there is a lot of criticism regarding the ad-libbed dialogue at the end of the film. Coppola had Brando improvised in character as they attempted to work out a suitable ending that dealt with the questions the film raised. I go back to those who think that a writer's job is dialogue. It is not the most important thing. The important thing is that Kurtz allows himself to be assassinated and passes on his rogue army to Willard. Willard has to choose light or darkness. He can walk away and make a choice about his own duality, or he can give in and go mad as Kurtz did. Whether or not you like the end of *Apocalypse Now*, it stands as a prime example of theme guiding the plot.

Coppola realized that Milius's ending was not sufficient for the film that he was making with Milius's script. It is an interesting film because so many of the memorable moments in *Apocalypse Now* come from John Milius. Colonel Kilgore and his Air Cavalry, the "I love the smell of napalm in the morning" speech, water skiing behind the boat, and the Playboy bunnies. These are all from Milius. As a collaborator, Coppola did to *Apocalypse Now* what he did with *The Godfather*—he brought out the thematic questions that were being raised and took the material from great plot and character to the next level. The thematic content is what makes these movies viewable multiple times, as you can "get more" out them with each viewing.

David Simon and Ed Burns's *The Wire* is critically acclaimed for the same reason. They didn't just set out to make a dynamic cops-and-robbers show; they sought to expose the problems of the modern American city through the lens of the cops and robbers. Their genius is that they did it within the context of an exciting and well-executed dramatic series. I say this with the understanding that most of its success has come after the series was wrapped and audiences could discover it on DVD or by other means. It was on the chopping block every season and needed time to find a bigger audience. Yet, because of the strong thematic elements running through the series the show stands up to repeat viewings and is constantly finding a new audience. The great characters and plotting are a big part of this, as well, but theme puts it over the top.

David Simon has explicitly stated that he is driven by theme and meaning. As a former journalist he is exploring the world, as he has seen it, through fiction. The richness of the work is derived from the themes that he is exploring. Entertainment and thought are not at odds with each other. The greatest and most entertaining works of fiction have a great balance of the two. It is what keeps us coming back to it. Shakespeare, for example.

> *"When you make a movie, always try to discover what the theme of the movie is in one or two words. Every time I made a film, I always knew what I thought the theme was, the core, in one word. In "The Godfather," it was succession. In "The Conversation," it was privacy. In "Apocalypse," it was morality. The reason it's important to have this is because most of the time what a director really does is make decisions. All day long: Do you want it to be long hair or short hair? Do you want a dress or pants? Do you want a beard or no beard? There are many times when you don't know the answer. Knowing what the theme is always helps you. I remember in "The Conversation," they brought all these coats to me, and they said: Do you want him to look like a detective, Humphrey Bogart? Do you want him to look like a blah blah blah. I didn't know, and said the theme is 'privacy' and chose the plastic coat you could see through. So knowing the theme helps you make a decision when you're not sure which way to go."*
>
> *– Francis Coppola*

I had a conversation with a writer who had abandoned two of his screenplays. The reason, he thought, was because he didn't work out an outline off the top and didn't know what his ending was going to be. There certainly could have been a lot of truth in that reason, but my feeling was that he was writing his story out of plot, going from one bit of plot to another. Had he identified his theme, he would have come up with the ideas that would solve his troubles. The ending should satisfy the theme and this can help the writer find his or her way through "the plot."

## CHARACTERS

Creating great characters is an essential part of storytelling. The audience wants to empathize with the characters on screen, and they want to experience that character's journey. We can only disappoint our audience with weak or vague characters. Screenwriters are at a huge disadvantage when it comes to characters, as we don't have the ability to tell the audience what a person is thinking or feeling. We rarely have the luxury of exploring their pasts or examining the many facets of that person's life. What we have as screenwriters are characters that are doing things and saying things, and we can't stray far from our narrative or the film will be dead in the water.

The first thing you should consider is "go big or go home." Make your characters larger-than-life and make them unique. In real life, no one wants to spend their time with boring people; that goes double for the time they spend watching a movie. Even quiet characters like Harry Caul in Coppola's *The Conversation* is given larger-than-life characteristics. Harry isn't just a good surveillance technician, he is the *best* surveillance man in the business. With this extraordinary ability comes a larger-than-life character flaw, as well—he is extremely paranoid. Consider poor little Frodo in *The Lord of the Rings*, who seems at first glance to be an "Everyman." But he is extraordinary because he is the *only* one who can carry the ring. His spirit is the most pure of anyone, so he, the most unlikely of heroes, must carry the burden of the ring.

Often screenwriters start with character archetypes that are easy and quick to establish. Take James Cameron's megahit *Avatar.* Cameron needed to quickly establish his characters and his world in order to keep the narrative flowing. He doesn't want to slow everything down to "establish character." The quick way into this is to establish the archetypes: the earnest, tough as nails scientist; the war loving Colonel; the geek scientist; the money grubbing corporate jerk; and the noble warriors. The use of the archetype allows Cameron to move the story along with speed.

The drawback to this is that the reviewers will refer to your characters as "cardboard cutouts" who are empty of originality. This drawback is very real and something the screenwriter needs to consider carefully. This is where the writer needs to go from the general to the specific. You might start with a general character that we have seen before but you need to create something more unique as the story unfolds.

Audiences are delighted by memorable characters. They might be real life people, like General George Patton and Richard Nixon, or they might be fictional, like Indiana Jones, Sam Spade, Vito Corleone, or Ellen Ripley. The other weapon in the screenwriter's arsenal is casting. Casting is one of the most important elements in fully realizing our characters. Consider the actors in the above roles: George C. Scott, Anthony Hopkins, Harrison

Ford, Humphrey Bogart, Marlon Brando, and Sigourney Weaver. These are the allies of the screenwriter, as they bring so much of their own personalities and strengths to any given role. The independent filmmaker is at an utter disadvantage when he or she is not able to secure name talent for a film. An A-List actor brings familiarity to a role and the audience doesn't have to work at getting to know and understand the character. There isn't a lot of time to establish character so securing known talent only helps a film. Often, actors are typecast for this very reason. It becomes a bit of a plug and play for any given movie.

Certainly no one would expect Tom Hanks to be given a role like Hannibal Lector. Gus Van Sant's utterly ridiculous remake of Alfred Hitchcock's *Psycho* is a great example of this, as Vince Vaughn was cast in the role of Norman Bates. I have nothing against Vaughn as an actor, but when you compare Anthony Perkins and Vaughn in the role, you can see the problem of miscasting a role. Vaughn is a fine actor, but he brings qualities to Norman Bates that don't ring true to the audience. Perkins was excellent at producing a somewhat creepy asexuality in the role of Norman Bates, and it translated into one of cinema's most memorable characters. Vaughn, despite his own talent, could not produce a memorable Norman Bates. This is the power of proper casting, as well as casting to type.

If you seek it out, you can see Tom Selleck's screen test for Indiana Jones. It is difficult to imagine Selleck as Indiana Jones because Harrison Ford brought his own characteristics to the role. I am certain that *Raiders of the Lost Ark* would have been a very fine film with Selleck in it, but it would be a different film. Both actors can play "vulnerable" very well, but Ford brought a more rugged and scruffy characteristic to the role that Selleck would not have. Even though they would have said the same lines and gone through the same actions, the film would have had a different tone and feeling.

One of the most important things that you can do for your characters is to make sure they have clear motivations. The motivations might not be clear to the audience at any given time, but your characters need to have their own goals. Jack Sparrow from *Pirates of the Caribbean* is a great example of a character who is very clearly motivated but doesn't give away what he wants. If fact, he lies, cheats, and steals, confusing the audience and other characters as to what his wants and needs are in the story. If you could praise the television series *Lost*, it would be that the series had two strongly motivated characters who hid their motives. John Locke and Sawyer were highlights of the series because the audience is never quite sure what they are up to and are often surprised when they reveal truth in their characters. The same can be said for Sgt. Sefton in Billy Wilder's *Stalag 17* (William Holden) or Christine in Wilder's *Witness for the Prosecution* (Marlene Dietrich). Often writers feel the need to reveal too much information, and there are times when the writer knows exactly what a character wants but holds back that information until the right moment.

The motivated character drives the plot and story. It is the wants and needs of those characters that moves the narrative forward. Many times, story logic problems come from flaws in this element. Often writers will have a predetermined plot and will connect the dots and not consider their characters. In an odd way your characters should start to talk to you. You may want the story to go a certain way, but once the character is established, it may start to feel dishonest. If you ignore this, then you will start to create logic problems in the story. The audience will come along for the ride until it starts to feel false. At that point, the writer reveals him or herself and the audience starts to feel like there is a manipulation going on rather than a story unfolding organically. This is the tough part of writing the film—making it feel like it isn't being written. If you look at the criticism hurled at George Lucas's prequels to the *Star Wars* films, you can see this problem clearly. Lucas had the predetermined ending of Anakin turning to the dark side and becoming Darth Vader, and this posed a real problem for the trilogy. What are Anakin's primary motivations? What causes him to go to the dark side? In criticism of the series, many have suggested that he was a brat who wasn't allowed to date the girl he wanted and was asked to be more disciplined by his mentor. How does this move the story forward to the inevitable ending? The films have a lot of plot, but character isn't the driving force. The first trilogy of films had very clearly defined goals: save the princess, escape the Empire, and disable the shield generator (and destroy the Death Star). The over complication of plot in the prequels ended up being mostly exposition and distraction. *The Empire Strikes Back* is the most episodic of the original films, but everyone has a clear goal: Luke is going to train to be a Jedi; and Leia, Han, and the others are trying to escape the clutches of Vader. Vader also has a clear goal: confront Skywalker and bring him to the dark side. As the most complicated of the first three films, the goals of the characters are clear. This cannot be said for the prequels, as they tie a lot of events together but are not pushed forward by the needs of the characters. Anakin does give into the dark side of the force, but the journey feels false. The audience doesn't empathize with him and his turn to the Emperor feels false and written. We see the writer writing.

Compare this to Michael Corleone in *The Godfather.* Michael transforms from an idealistic young war hero to the ruthless head of a Mafia family. His transformation feels honest because it is based in character. Michael might say he is not like his father—and it is true, he lacks his father's capacity for kindness and strength. He is much more conniving and ruthless, and he pays lip service to his father's ideal of family even as he destroys it. At the beginning of the film, his motivation is to protect his father, and he murders a cop and rival Mafioso to achieve that. After his brother is murdered and he returns to America, Michael becomes the head of the family and, despite his idealistic views, he is drawn into power and control and he loses himself and his family. This is the realm of tragedy, where the protagonist fails because of a fatal flaw. The only problem with *The Godfather,* as reviewers pointed out when it was released, is that Michael doesn't suffer. Othello and Macbeth suffer, but Michael seems to succeed. Francis Coppola and Mario Puzo do address this criticism in their masterpiece sequel to the film. In the end, Michael does suffer. Comparing *The Godfather* films and the *Star Wars* prequels may seem unfair, but in terms of character and story, the function is the same. You don't need to excuse one as drama and the other as an action film. All films are written under the same principles.

One pitfall to look out for is adding characters to provide exposition that explains the story. You need to evaluate that character's place in the story. So often a character is added to be a vocal sounding board for the protagonist since we don't know what he or she is thinking. I return to *Inception* here and Ariadne (Ellen Page). Her motivation in the story is fairly weak. She wants the job as the architect. But why? Why does she *need* this job? What happens if she doesn't get it? What is her prime motivation? Her place in the story often feels like an expositional tool in the hands of the writer. This doesn't ruin the film for the audience, but it does become a flaw and a missed opportunity for a great character. Often I read screenplays that feature a protagonist and his or her friend, and the friend is just there for the purpose of information. Your job as a writer isn't to give out information but to create drama and tension. What does that other character want that is an obstacle to your protagonist? What are they providing the story in terms of conflict? What do they want for themselves?

Look at a film like *Jaws* as a great example of well-defined main characters, each having a stake in the outcome of the plot.

CHIEF BRODY. Brody is the protagonist with a clean line of action; shut down the beach and protect the citizens of Amity against the shark attacks

JAWS. Jaws is the antagonist of the film. He wants to use the beaches of Amity as breakfast, lunch, and dinner.

MAYOR VAUGHAN. A clear obstacle to the goals of Chief Brody. The tourist season is about to start and the Mayour needs the beaches open for the economy of Amity. He holds power over Brody.

HOOPER. Hooper is a marine biologist who has a keen interest in sharks. The unbelievable size of Jaws keeps him in Amity and he becomes an ally to Brody.

QUINT. Quint is a local fisherman who will kill the shark for a large bounty. He wants to be paid handsomely for killing Jaws. He has a personal, secret, vendetta against sharks.

There is a wonderful simplicity to all of this. What each character wants or needs is very clear, but the opposition to or difference between those goals is what makes the story so dynamic. The stakes are high for everyone involved. The shark is killing the citizens and tourists, but Amity needs the tourist money to survive the winter.

Each character is endowed with very specific traits that, with the help of great actors, creates a great deal of empathy in the audience. Chief Brody is afraid of the water. Hooper is arrogant but brilliant. The Mayor is a greedy, beady-eyed politician. Quint is just plain nuts. And Jaws is the biggest great white shark known to man. You might say that the characters are fairly thin and archetypal, and I would agree. However, this doesn't make the movie a bad movie. I would argue that most genre films don't have deep, three-dimensional characters. The weakness lies in the medium rather than the writers or filmmakers being at fault. This goes back to my point about the importance of casting. When you put Roy Scheider, Robert Shaw, Richard Dreyfuss and Murray Hamilton in a film together, good things happen. The actors are typecast but this typecasting helps the audience to quickly associate and empathize with or dislike the characters. It is a form of shorthand. Again, those more specific traits that I outlined above help to give the characters a uniqueness that separates them from other roles they have played. Scheider is different here than in *The French Connection* or *Marathon Man*. It is still Scheider, but we can buy him as Chief Brody, the police officer who left the city to police an island, despite his fear of the water.

## STRUCTURE

David Mamet has provided a simple exercise that will help in writing your drama. He says you need to ask yourself three basic questions:

"Who wants what from whom or who wants what?"

"What happens if he doesn't get it?"

"Why now?"

This is the simplest method I have read that sums up what the writer needs to do to have a drama with motivated characters and proper tension. You should ask yourself this of your overall story as well as all of your scenes.

Take, for example, *The Bourne Identity*. What does Bourne want? He wants to remember who he is. What happens if he doesn't get it? He is not whole as a human being. Why now? During a botched assassination attempt, he lost his memory. This is the overall arc of the story. He needs to know what happened and who he really is, something that is easy for the audience to empathize with. In terms of the story, he now has to navigate what it means to find out his identity. The first clue is a Swiss bank account. He needs to get to Switzerland to find out what this means. When he gets there, his obstacle to getting what he wants is an active CIA who is trying to kill him. This is the opposing goal. When Bourne discovers the safety deposit box he realizes that it provides more questions than answers. He has many identities on several passports. He chooses the first passport and decides to go to Paris to find the truth there. The obstacle is still the relentless pursuit by the CIA. He needs a car, so he offers money to a woman to give him a ride. Why does she help him? Because she is broke and motivated to help herself despite the danger that Bourne poses. Without this element of her desperation, there is no motivation to help and she might as well turn him in. If she isn't in a state of complete desperation, the audience won't buy the logic.

Most young writers neglect the third question. "Why Now?" They ignore it because it is a very hard question to answer and it requires a lot of thought and planning. Yet, so much tension is given to the story when you answer it properly. When Luke Skywalker is asked by Ben Kenobi to go to Alderaan with him, Skywalker refuses because of the needs of his uncle and the farm. How does Lucas make it so that Luke goes on this journey with Kenobi? The Storm Troopers tracing the Droids kill his aunt and uncle and burn down the farm. Luke has no reason to stay. Why now? Because Leia is going to be executed (high stakes), and there is nothing preventing him from going.

Even in silly comedies, the writers come up with the answer to why it is so imperative that the characters act now. In *Superbad,* the goal of the protagonist(s) is to get the booze to the party.

Why now? Because it is their last chance at getting the girls before they all disband for college. Harold and Kumar need to get to White Castle because it is the only thing that will satisfy their drug-induced munchies. In *Planes, Trains and Automobiles,* Neil has to get home to spend Thanksgiving with his family. These are not heavy ideas, but they create the tension for the audience. It is the idea of the ticking bomb—the audience is aware that at a certain point the protagonist isn't going to succeed because there is only so much time available. So they sit in anticipation.

This is also called the "or-else factor." The protagonist must achieve the goal or-else. Frodo must destroy the ring *or-else* the world will fall into darkness and all will be lost. Luke must save the Princess *or-else* the Empire will rule the Universe. What is the cost of failure? The higher the cost, the greater the tension. This is "the stakes."

> *"A movie has to have a great opening. It must command attention… You don't ever want to open a play at the top of your bent. But a movie should open at the top of its bent, it must, because this damn thing (points to the screen) is dead. The only living thing are the people sitting out here. It's a projected image, and you cannot bring the thing alive unless you seize the people at the beginning. The rider-less horse has to come in." – Orson Welles.*

Billy Wilder said the writer needs to grab the audience by the throat and never let them go. This is even truer in the modern day, as the audience is often at home and has the ability to change the channel or stream a different film. You have a limited amount of time to win over the audience and leave them wanting to know what is going to happen next. When David Mamet wrote the screenplay for *Glengarry Glen Ross*, based on his own play, he added a new scene at the beginning. In the scene Mamet introduces a new character, Blake (Alec Baldwin), who has been sent by the downtown bosses to lay down the law on a group of real estate salesmen. He sets up the stakes of the film right away, sell some real estate or you are fired. Here Mamet shows a clear understanding of the needs of the motion picture over what is required in the theater. The clean line of action is established and the audience is immediately engaged.

When you consider the films of Welles and Wilder—those giving the advice—you will see that they don't just pay lip service to the idea of immediate audience engagement. Wilder's *Double Indemnity* starts with a shot up Walter Neff confessing his sins into a recording device for his friend Keys, the insurance investigator. Joe Gillis lies dead, face down in a pool, in *Sunset Boulevard*. Joe and Jerry witness the St. Valentine's Day massacre and need to run from the mob in *Some Like it Hot*. Charles Foster Kane utters "Rosebud" as he dies in the opening of *Citizen Kane*. In Welles's version of *Othello*, he invents a scene in which Desdemona and Othello are being carried in a funeral procession while the villain Iago is being hoisted up in a cage. In Welles *Touch of Evil*, a bomb is planted in the back of a car in one of cinema's greatest single shots. The bomb explodes and Welles has the audience's attention.

What is interesting in *Sunset Boulevard* is that you could leave out the fact that Gillis is a man narrating from the grave. Wilder could have held that information back from the audience and had fun shocking them with his unexpected death at the end of the film. Instead he, and his writing partners, Charles Brackett and D.M. Marshman Jr., decided to start with the image of Gillis dead in the pool. Instead of easing the audience into the narrative, Wilder grabs them by the throat.

George Lucas and Steven Spielberg both made their mark following this advice. The opening of *Raiders of the Lost Ark* is a thrilling action sequence. Indiana Jones faces death as he tries to retrieve a golden idol. *Star Wars* begins with a space battle. In *Jaws*, a shark mutilates the young swimmer.

*Star Wars* is a good example of Lucas "buying time" with his audience. If he doesn't start with a bang, then he has a very long buildup of exposition, and the audience will become restless and bored. Once the droids land on Tatooine, there is a slow build of story and character that lasts for more than half an hour. Exciting the audience right off the top allows him to spend time building his characters and developing story (exposition). This is also a science fiction film, so there is a learning curve for the audience as they get to know the world of the film. A strong start that grabs the audience by the throat affords the filmmaker time with the audience with the promise of bigger things to come.

> *"Get your man up a tree. In the second act throw stones at him. In the third act get him down out of the tree." –*
> *George M. Cohan*

Generally films are thought to have what is called a three-act structure, a beginning, middle, and end. In the most simplistic sense, it has been described as "Get your hero up a tree, throw stones at him, then get him down." There is a lot of analysis regarding the three-act structure, but in my experience, the acts tend to work themselves out naturally. If you are competent enough to create a character with a goal and an antagonist with an opposing goals, then you will work it out naturally.

> *"I think any sane person resists the idea that there is a formal and ineffable structure to films, which is what the Americans have diagnosed as the 'three-act' structure. They'll talk about the problems in the second act, problems in the third act. It seems to me to be absurd that such a liquid form should be calcified into three acts." – Anthony Minghella*

There will be many people that balk at this Minghella quote, but if you explore the ideas of structure, you will find many different approaches. Whatever works for you is my answer. The important thing is that you have the audience caring about your characters and wondering what is going to happen next. If you do this, then you are doing your job. Minghella's mention of the fluid nature of the story is very apparent in three of his most successful films *The English Patient*, *The Talented Mr. Ripley* and *Cold Mountain*. All three of these films work on their own internal structure. *The Talented Mr. Ripley* is the closest the film-maker comes to conventional narrative, but—like Coppola and *The Conversation*—Minghella is more interested in the character study than the plot. The film often feels like a conventional thriller but is subversive and the rhythm of the story is broken by Minghella's interest in Tom Ripley and what makes him tick. In going back to theme, Minghella is driven by the idea stated by Tom at the beginning of the film, "It's better to be a fake somebody than a real nobody." This theme drives the narrative.

There is nothing wrong with following a guide for structure, but my feeling is, again, it will work itself out. This is the natural part of storytelling. For example, if you were to tell a friend at work about your disastrous trip into the office today, you would start at the beginning, move to the middle, and finish at the end. You might say that you slept in and decided to take the highway with the goal of getting to work on time. On the way, a car cut you off and you almost veered into the guardrail. You might state that you honked at the other driver, who went into a fit of road rage. The person listening to your story will ask, "What happened next?" You say that you called emergency and after a couple of close calls, the police intervened. How did it end? They arrested the offender who stunk of alcohol. They took your information, and you got to work two hours late.

The structure of this "story" is quite natural to us. The character has a goal—getting to work (beginning). What is stopping him? A road rage incident that almost causes a fatal accident (middle). What was the resolution? The police show up and the character averts disaster, getting to work late but in one piece (end). Structure is the natural evolution of a story.

Each scene of your film should also contain this similar structure. A character shows up at the beginning of a scene with a need. The middle of the scene is the opposition to that need. The end of the scene will have the character getting what her or she needs or it will present a new direction for that character to take.

## FROZEN AND THE ART OF MISDIRECTION

I have seen Disney's *Frozen* several times now. As a father of twin girls, it is impossible to escape. I've seen the movie and now the ice skating show, too. I've played the CD in the car. It was the first movie the girls saw in a movie theater. You would think I would be sick of it by now, but oddly enough, I am not. The last few times I have been subjected to it, my thoughts have gone to how well-constructed the film is.

One thing my little preschoolers have always been afraid of is "the bad guy." The villains in most films terrify my daughters, so we have stayed in the realm of preschool entertainment, where the stakes are low and the drama gentle. They are starting to grow out of this, but we aren't there yet. *Frozen* appeals to little kids because the antagonist, Elsa, is a sympathetic villain (if we can call her that). She has powers she cannot control, and the bad things she does are done out of fear and not desire. There are other "bad guys" in the film, such as the Duke of Weselton and, in a surprise ending (spoilers here for those who are residing under a rock), Prince Hans. We will get to Hans in a moment. Elsa also creates the gigantic snowman called Marshmallow to guard her.

The clean line of action in *Frozen* is to unfreeze what has been frozen. Ana, the protagonist, must find her sister and bring her back to the kingdom to achieve this goal. Along the way, she meets her companions on this quest: a snowman called Olaf (comic relief); as well as a skilled outdoorsman and his reindeer, Kristoff and Sven. During this quest, Elsa accidentally strikes Ana's heart with her powers, and it is said that only an act of true love can save her from becoming, well, frozen. This brings me to the clever way that the script misdirects the audience. It coaches the mind to think in a very particular way.

In the first act of the film, Ana meets Prince Hans and they instantly fall in love. After the coronation ceremony crowning Elsa Queen, Ana and Hans decide they want to marry. Ana asks Elsa's permission for the marriage but Elsa rejects her. An argument ensues, and with what becomes the inciting incident in the film, Elsa accidentally uses her magical powers and sets off an eternal winter. Elsa escapes to the mountains, not realizing what she has done. Later in the film, when she strikes Ana with her powers, it is said that only an act of true love will heal her frozen heart. First of all, this sets up a time frame. Ana must get to Hans or she will die. This bodes well for a third act climax. It also causes anxiety in the audience.

When Ana finally gets to Hans for her kiss, he reveals what his motives are in the story. He only wanted to marry her so he could become King. He is twelfth in line for the throne in his own family, so he is just trying to jump the queue, so to speak. The audience discovers that Hans is really a villain. His goal wasn't to marry the sweet Princess Ana but to stage a coup, in which he planned to marry Ana, kill Elsa, and take control of the kingdom. This little twist at the end is quite good, and even I got suckered into falling for it, despite the fact that I am usually good at detecting these things. So how did they set it up? How did writer/director Jennifer Lee fool us?

There are a few things at play here. The first is the screenplay itself, which I will get to in a moment. The second thing is our own prejudices, for lack of a better word. When the idea is an act of true love will heal, most people automatically assume that this is referring to romantic love. Especially at the movies. But when Ana (spoilers again, you rock dwellers) saves her sister from being killed by Hans and, in so doing, puts Elsa's life ahead of her own, we learn that the love that heals is not romantic love at all, but is instead familial love—the love shared between family members. It is a clever dupe. Because we are conditioned to think of love as romantic love, we don't see this plot twist coming. Even when Kristoff shows up in the big climax, we are still thinking that he must be her true love! It's Disney working against its own clichés, and it works wonderfully. As Mamet says, "surprising yet inevitable" (he attributes this to Aristotle).

The smart thing about the screenplay is that Jennifer Lee doesn't just trust that we will be suckered in by our own preconceptions. She makes sure to solidify the idea over and over again to make certain that the audience is thinking in the way she wants them to think. Several times in the film this comes up.

In the song "In the First Time in Forever" Ana sings about

finding her true love. "For the first time in forever. I'm getting what I'm dreaming of—a chance to leave my sister's world a chance to find true love".

Then Ana falls for Hans and asks Elsa for her blessing on the marriage.

*ELSA*

*. . . You can't marry a man you just met.*

*ANNA*

*You can if it's true love.*

*ELSA*

*Anna, what do you know about true love?*

*ANNA*

*More than you. All you know is how to shut people out.*

*ELSA*

*You asked for my blessing, but my answer is no.*

Then she meets Kristoff on her journey to find Elsa and tells him about Hans:

*KRISTOFF*

*Didn't your parents ever warn you about strangers?*

*Anna eyes Kristoff up and down, then slides away from him.*

*ANNA*

*Yes, they did . . . But Hans is not a stranger.*

*KRISTOFF*

*Oh yeah? What's his last name?*

*ANNA*

*. . . Of-the-Southern-Isles?*

*KRISTOFF*

*What's his favorite food?*

*ANNA*

*. . . Sandwiches.*

*KRISTOFF*

*Best friend's name?*

*ANNA*

*Probably John.*

*KRISTOFF*

*Eye color.*

*ANNA*

*Dreamy.*

*KRISTOFF*

*Foot size . . . ?*

*ANNA*

*Foot size doesn't matter.*

*KRISTOFF*

*Have you had a meal with him yet? What if you hate
the way he eats?*

*What if you hate the way he picks his nose?*

*ANNA*

*Picks his nose?*

*KRISTOFF*

*And eats it.*

*ANNA*

*Excuse me, sir. He's a prince.*

*KRISTOFF*

*All men do it.*

*ANNA*

*Ew. Look it doesn't matter; it's true love.*

*KRISTOFF*

*Doesn't sound like true love.*

*ANNA*

*Are you some sort of love expert?*

*KRISTOFF*

*No. But I have friends who are.*

*ANNA*

*You have friends who are love experts. . . . I'm not buying it.*

The love experts stuff is a setup for later in the film. Then, as they are being chased down by wolves:

*A wolf jumps at them, but Kristoff kicks it off.*

*KRISTOFF*

*Who marries a man she just met?*

*Anna grabs the lute, swings it right at Kristoff's head.*

*ANNA*

*It's true love!*

*He screams, as she. . . . BAM! . . . swings past Kristoff
and knocks a wolf away.*

*KRISTOFF*

*(shocked) Whoa.*

*Just then Kristoff is yanked off the sled by another wolf.
The torch goes flying. Anna catches it, shocked.*

*ANNA*

*Christopher!*

*Kristoff grabs onto a loose rope hanging from the back
of the sled and holds on for dear life as he's dragged
behind.*

*KRISTOFF*

*It's Kristoff!*

Not only does Anna reinforce the idea of Hans and true love,
she diminishes the idea that she might fall in love with Kristoff
as she doesn't even know his name. Anna eventually meets the
love experts, who turn out to be Trolls. Kristoff thinks they can
heal Ana's frozen heart, but they are unable to—only an act of
true love can save her. In the last song of the film, the Trolls try
to get Kristoff and Ana together, but again, the idea is put forward
that Hans is her true love. We have no reason to doubt this as
we have been told as much over and over again.

GRAND PABBIE (CONT'D)

Anna, your life is in danger. There is ice in your heart, put there by your sister. If not removed, to solid ice will you freeze, forever.

ANNA

What...? No.

KRISTOFF

So remove it, Grand Pabbie.

GRAND PABBIE

I can't. If it was her head, that would be easy. But only an act of true love can thaw a frozen heart.

ANNA

An act of true love?

BULDA

(googley, to her hubby)

A true love's kiss, perhaps?

A bunch of trolls give each other kisses.

Anna shivers again, collapsing into Kristoff's arms. More of her hair turns white.

KRISTOFF

Anna, we've got to get you back to Hans.

ANNA

(still weak) . . . Hans.

*KRISTOFF*

*Help us out, Sven.*

*Kristoff grabs Sven's antlers. Sven pulls them out.*

*Kristoff helps Anna onto Sven and hops up behind her.*

*KRISTOFF (CONT'D)*

*Come on, Olaf!*

*Sven takes off. Olaf grabs Sven's tail, rides with them.*

*OLAF*

*I'm coming! Let's go kiss Hans! Who is this Hans?!*

*Eventually Ana makes her way to Hans.*

*Hans rushes to Anna. She falls into his arms.*

*HANS (CONT'D)*

*You're so cold.*

*ANNA*

*(weak, but desperate)*

*Hans, you have to kiss me.*

*HANS*

*What?*

*ANNA*

*Now. Here we go.*

*She tries to kiss him, but is too weak to pull herself up
in his arms.*

*GERDA*

*We'll give you two some privacy.*

*Everyone shuffles out, leaving Hans and Anna alone.*

*HANS*

*What happened out there?*

*ANNA*

*Elsa struck me with her powers.*

*HANS*

*You said she'd never hurt you.*

*ANNA*

*I was wrong.*

*Anna crumbles, weak.*

*HANS*

*Anna.*

*Hans carries her to a couch, sets her down.*

*ANNA*

*(shivering more)*

*She froze my heart and only an act of true love can save me.*

*HANS*

*(understanding)*

*A true love's kiss.*

*He takes her chin in his hand and gives her a tender smile. He leans in slowly . . . gently. . . . Then he stops.*

*HANS (CONT'D)*

*Oh, Anna. If only there was someone out there who loved you.*

ANNA

What?

Hans gets up, leaving her there.

ANNA (CONT'D)

. . .You said you did.

He goes to the window and shuts the curtains.

HANS

As thirteenth in line in my own kingdom, I didn't stand
a chance. I knew I'd have to marry into the
throne somewhere—

ANNA

What are you talking about?

HANS

(putting out the candles)

As heir, Elsa was preferable, of course. But no one was
getting anywhere with her. But you–

ANNA

Hans?

HANS

You were so desperate for love you were willing to
marry me, just like that. Hans crosses the room, grabs a
pitcher of water from a table and goes to the fireplace.

HANS (CONT'D)

I figured, after we married, I'd have to stage a little
accident for Elsa.

*Hans pours the water on the fireplace, putting out the fire. Anna tries to stop him. She falls to the floor, weak.*

And the surprise is revealed. Now the audience, who have grown fond of Kristoff, hope that he can get back in time to save her. It is a very clever bit of writing. Also, the behavior in the scene is running parallel to the dialogue. Not only is Hans revealing himself through dialogue, he is putting out the fires to ensure her certain death. He pulls closed the curtains, snubs the candles (all of which makes me think of the murder of Desdemona in Othello), and douses the fireplace.

Now this doesn't mean that every film needs a "twist ending." Every great film needs a satisfying ending. Sometimes when you start working towards a twist, you end up putting the cart before the horse. You end up manipulating your story so much that you start to break logic and the audience begins to lose interest. So when the twist finally happens, you get a big sigh and a "meh." A film needs to work first, without the twist. And when the new information arises—information that one character has been dishonest with us—the surprise happens and the audience is delighted. One of the most famous examples of this is *The Sixth Sense*. The film works just fine without the twist ending, but it wowed audiences when they found out the truth of what they were watching. The only trouble that M. Night Shyamalan got into was trying to replicate that moment in subsequent films. Not all endings need to be twist endings, they just need to be satisfying.

## KNOW THE RULES AND BREAK THEM

Most of the examples I have used throughout this book have been commercial and genre-based films. I use these examples as they illustrate very clearly how adherence to the rules of storytelling can help the writer find success. Learning these rules gives you the power to control your narrative. But what about breaking those rules?

I have neglected a lot of classics because so many of them play around with these so-called "rules." The films of Stanley Kubrick don't march to the same beat of the drum. Kubrick was an artist whose intent went beyond providing an entertaining narrative. The opening of *2001*, although visually arresting, doesn't set up a protagonist and his or her goals. It is conceptual and thematic. It plants an idea in the mind of the audience. *A Clockwork Orange* doesn't present us with a protagonist we want to root for. It is a brutal film with intentions outside of "spinning a yarn." *Full Metal Jacket* neglects the three-act structure, being episodic rather than a straight narrative with a "clean line of action."

The highly acclaimed classic "The Godfather" begins with a big wedding, where we are introduced to the characters and the world of the film, but the story doesn't actually begin until Don Corleone is gunned down over forty-five minutes into the film. Up to that point, the movie has been developing characters and story, but the audience doesn't know where it is all leading until the Don is shot and Michael is forced into action to save his father. Interestingly, because the film is called *The Godfather,* the suggestion seems to be that Marlon Brando's character is the protagonist of the film. In fact, Michael is the protagonist, and the journey that we follow is his. Brando is given a great deal of early screen time, which helps the audience create an emotional attachment to him, leading to a much greater impact when he is almost assassinated. If this were to happen earlier, then the audience might not care as much, and the narrative wouldn't have the power that it does.

Frank Capra's classic, *It's a Wonderful Life,* starts with the backstory of the character George Bailey (Jimmy Stewart). The inciting incident happens when Bailey's uncle loses the bank's money. As a result, the Bailey Building and Loan and George Bailey's world are in ruins. George is about to jump off the bridge one hour and forty minutes into a two hour and ten minute film. This is an huge amount of time for the audience to wait to see where the film is going and to discover the central goal of the protagonist. All of this with voice-over narration from the angels.

In the modern cinema, Terry Gilliam and David Lynch are notorious for their lack of interest in conventional narrative. Both filmmakers revel in atmosphere and visual splendor. Again, their primary interest does not lie in telling a traditional story, but both are adept at doing so. Terry Gilliam's *The Fisher King* is his most accessible work, as is Lynch's *The Straight Story* (an appropriate title). It should be noted that Gilliam and Lynch did not write these films. *The Fisher King* was written by Richard LaGravenese and *The Straight Story* was penned by John Roach and Mary Sweeney.

Charles Laughton's horror, fantasy, nightmare *The Night of the Hunter* divides audiences and critics because it has some very distinct shifts in tone. The film starts off as a straight horror film and then turns into a twisted comedic nightmare fantasy. Laughton and writer James Agee adapted the novel by Davis Grubb, and it is clear that Laughton chose this film for reasons beyond a good story. The film is an indictment of religious hypocrisy.

The film starts off rather conventionally, with a man hiding stolen money with his impoverished children before being taken to prison for theft and murder. While in prison he meets a preacher, who becomes very interested in the lost money. The man is executed, and when the preacher gets out, he goes to the family to steal the money. The point of view of the film is from the young protagonist John Harper. His goal in the story is to protect the stolen money and his little sister from the Preacher, Harry Powell. This idea seems conventional enough, and the first part of the film plays out like a horror/thriller. In the second act, John's mother is murdered by the preacher, and he must take his sister and run. This brings us to an extremely surreal and expressionistic boat trip down the river with the preacher giving chase over land. The film's tone switches to a nightmare fantasy and then, with the introduction of Rachel Cooper, the film turns sharply to dark comedy. An undeniably strange film, it is Laughton's interest in the themes of the film that drives it into unconventional territory. The familiar beats of a horror/thriller are altered by the filmmaker's interest in something more than just the narrative plot.

In Francis Coppola's masterpiece, *The Conversation*, he disguises a character study in the form of a thriller. The film has a straightforward plot: a surveillance expert, Harry Caul, is hired to record the conversation of a man and a woman in the middle of a busy outdoor square in the middle of lunch hour. He says at the beginning what he wants. He wants a big fat recording. He wants his pay for a job well done. When he goes to hand in the recording to his corporate client, "the Director," an abrasive subordinate played by a young Harrison Ford meets him. Caul's instructions are to deliver the recordings to the Director, not a subordinate, and being a consummate professional, as well as an extremely paranoid person, he refuses the money from the subordinate. Caul will only deliver the recording to the Director. Curious about the strong reaction from the subordinate, Caul revisits the recordings only to uncover new dialogue from the couple, in which they say, "He'd kill us if he had the chance." The intimidating and suspicious behavior of the subordinate, who has a clear goal of getting the tapes, causes Caul to withhold the recordings. His want of money is replaced by his want of not having this couple's blood on his hands. This story is original, and on first glance it doesn't feel unconventional, as thrillers go. What makes it more unconventional and rule-breaking is Coppola's primary interest, Harry Caul. Coppola knows he needs a compelling plot and narrative to keep the audience's interest, but he seems centrally interested in the character of Harry Caul and the themes of privacy and surveillance. Caul is a brilliant man who has cut himself off from human contact. He is the product of his work—a highly paranoid man, suspicious of other people's interests. A line of dialogue that is repeated as a motif in the film is from the woman under surveillance. "I always think that he was once somebody's baby boy. Really, I do. I think he was once somebody's baby boy, and he had a mother and a father who loved him, and now there he is, half dead on a park bench, and where are his mother or his father, all his uncles now?" This is a theme that occurs many times in Coppola's work. Whether it is Michael Corleone, isolated and alone at the end of *The Godfather*, Harry Caul, whose "girlfriend" doesn't know where he lives, Dracula, longing for his long lost love, Elizabeta, or Dominic, who has wasted his life in search of his life's work in *Youth Without Youth*. Coppola has an acute interest in the character of Harry Caul and the themes that are revealed in the film. And that is where the film starts to work in unconventional ways.

Coppola introduces Caul's girlfriend early in the film. Caul pays her a visit on his birthday, presumably for a sexual encounter. While they are getting intimate, she inquires about where he lives and starts to ask him personal questions. He gets angry and eventually leaves her. In a conventional film narrative, this character of the lover would have to come back into the plot later in the movie. In *The Conversation*, this is the only scene where you see her. Caul attempts to call her later on but is unsuccessful. Much later in the film, a new character is introduced. Bernie Moran is another surveillance expert who has come into town for a surveillance convention. Moran lives in the shadow of Caul's greatness. They meet at the convention, and eventually, everyone goes back to Caul's office for a little party. Moran comes into the film as a jealous competitor late in the narrative, and once the party is done, he no longer plays a part in the film. He does provide some exposition about Harry, in which the audience learns that Caul once did a surveillance job that ended in the murder of his targets. The guilt stemming from this previous job is the motivation for Harry Caul to withhold his recordings from the Director.

There are sequences in this film that don't move the narrative forward. There is a dream sequence where Caul speaks to the woman he thinks is going to be murdered. There is a conversation and relationship with a model who had manned Moran's booth at the convention. All of these moments in the film fly in the face of "the rules" but are put there on purpose. They give the character more nuance and unique definition, while also serving to help develop the themes of the film.

Coppola understands the requirements of a "thriller" genre film, and he uses its narrative devices to keep the audience in a degree of suspense and mystery, but he deviates from the genre for the sake of his other interests. *The Conversation* remains one of the most cinematic of films. The story revolves around media (the recordings), point of view, and perception. It allows the audience to experience the narrative as Harry Caul encounters it. The audience, like Caul, is trying to put the puzzle together.

The film was partly inspired by Michelangelo Antonioni's unconventional film *Blow-Up*. Antonioni defied narrative "rules" and attempted to discover a new cinematic language and structure for telling stories on film. Coppola plays with these unconventional techniques but does provide the audience with more accessible conventional storytelling techniques so as to not exclude those who have come to see a "movie." Another film that was inspired by Antonioni's *Blow-Up* is Brian De Palma's 1981 thriller *Blow Out*. It is very interesting to compare these three films, as Coppola's film—as well as De Palma's—are homages to Antonioni's cinematic idea, and each film bring a different sensibility and personal subversion.

*Blow-Up* is the story of "the Photographer," who photographs an intimate couple in a London park, and after developing the photographs, begins to think he has photographed the murder of the man. This paranoid assertion is furthered by the woman's insistence on getting the film negatives from him. What is essentially cinematic about this idea is that it is based on what the character *sees* and, thus, what the audience sees. Like *Rear Window*, the audience only knows what the Photographer knows, as there are no scenes where that character isn't present. We see his point of view, and the conclusions we come to are similar to those that he comes to. The story is a mystery and the audience is a participant in it. What sets *Blow-Up* apart from traditional mysteries is Antonioni's breaking of narrative convention. The film has some elements of a regular thriller, but there are many digressions and loose ends. At one point the

Photographer takes a break from photographing his models, whom he refers to as "the birds," and takes a trip to the local pawn shop. He purchases a propeller and has it delivered to his studio. None of this serves the narrative at all. The pawnshop doesn't mean anything to the plot and neither does the propeller. If the goal was to get the Photographer to the park then this sideshow digression is considered weak. What drives him to go to the pawnshop? What does he need? How does this lead him to the park to photograph the secretive couple? In conventional narrative, this doesn't work. The propeller doesn't push the story forward, and it doesn't have any kind of payoff later on. But *Blow-Up* isn't interested in conventional narrative. The film splits the modern audience in two—on one side is that part of the audience that loves the film and its existential interests; on the other are those that find it an utter bore with no redeeming value. Antonioni dresses his film up as a mystery thriller but has an interest outside of the loose plot. He makes a film with a protagonist who is unlikable and misogynistic, and a plot that meanders along. Audiences of the day (1966) were titillated by the sexual threesome the photographer engages in with a couple of "birds" and seemed to be genuinely interested in the murder. Was it a real murder or something imagined? After all, the more the Photographer blows up the images, the less clear they become. This seems to be what Antonioni was most interested in—the form itself. The film is not about his character or his moral and ethical position, but rather, it is about how images are so subjective and ambiguous.

*The Conversation* has some of the same interests, and Coppola cleverly changes the idea from a visual idea (the photographs) to an aural idea (sound recording). "He'd kill us if he had the chance" is the line spoken in the film that makes Harry Caul apprehensive about handing over his recordings. The very fact that Antonioni names his characters "the Photographer" and "the Birds" tells us something about his interest in his characters. Coppola's *The Conversation* is much more of a character study than Antonioni's. He is interested in Harry Caul and how the surveillance lifestyle informs the character flaws of his protagonist. Harry Caul is not a warm person, and while the audience may admire his abilities, he is ultimately flawed and difficult to like. Yet there are aspects of the film's themes that are accessible to the audience, and Coppola does provide a payoff with a surprise twist that lovers of genre films can appreciate. Having said that, despite the success of *The Godfather*, *The Conversation* was not successful financially, even though it did extremely well critically and earned Coppola a nomination for best picture, along with his nomination for *The Godfather Part II*. "Breaking the rules" may have compromised the film financially. Coppola digresses with scenes that don't seem to advance the story as much as they advance our understanding of character. I will not divulge the surprise twist ending, but I will point out that it has a great deal to do with the point of view of the character. Like *Blow-Up*, we only see the film from the point of view of the protagonist, and we have to interpret what information we get just as he does. We experience the film through Harry Caul's point of view.

Brian De Palma's *Blow Out* is another homage to *Blow-Up*, with a nod to *The Conversation*. *Blow Out* is a smart movie but has the most conventional narrative of the three films. This isn't to knock the the film but simply to highlight the way these filmmakers approached their films. *Blow Out* stars John Travolta as a soundman for the movies. One night he is out gathering sound effects, and he happens to record and witness a car crash. It turns out that a leading presidential candidate is killed when his car loses control from a punctured tire and plunges into a river. Even though the film has a fairly conventional approach to plot, De Palma manages to sneak in his own personal obsessions of conspiracy and government corruption. De Palma employs a bravura visual style that you don't see in *The Conversation* or *Blow-Up*. He uses unconventional visual techniques, such as forced deep focus, split screen effects, and bold camera moves. These techniques heighten the emotional elements of the film. He also breaks out of the point of view of the other films, allowing the audience to get a third person point of view, from which the audience learns things that the protagonist has no knowledge of. Hitchcock does this visually in *Rear Window*, showing us some things that Jeffrey doesn't see while asleep at the window. De Palma steps out much further and gives the audience a significantly greater understanding of the story than that of the main character's understanding.

Conventional wisdom would suggest that De Palma's film was the most financially successful, as it is the most "accessible" and "conventional." However, ironically, *Blow-Up* turned out to be the most financially successful of the three films. This was due mostly to timing. Young audiences of the 1960s and 1970s were excited by the New Wave films coming out of Europe, feeling that Hollywood had lost touch with audiences and was not keeping up with new trends. *Blow-Up* also featured an orgy scene with The Photographer and two "birds," which drew a lot of attention to the film, as did the central mystery of the photographs themselves. There was a lot of discussion about what was seen in the photographs, which speaks to the power of the audience's experience of the film. De Palma's film was the least financially successful of the three, at least from the standpoint of budget-to-box-office success. I am not quite sure why this is, but it didn't find an audience in its day, despite a potboiler plot and great performances by Travolta and Allen. The film's lack of success may have stemmed for a very dark ending. Who knows? All three films hold up quite well, although young people today seem fairly hostile towards *Blow-Up* for its lack of clarity and narrative drive.

Breaking the rules can run the risk of fragmenting your audience, and in the end, it is up to the writer to understand the rules and what it means to break them. In the final analysis, what is most important is that that you do not write for the marketplace, but write for yourself. You need to make your film true to itself. If the theme or characters demand that you tell your story a certain way, go for it. Despite the lack of financial success of some of these rule-breakers, the writers still got paid. Keep in mind that many commercially designed films have failed to find an audience too. Stay passionate about your work. There are many films that didn't do well financially in their own time that are classics today. This list includes *It's a Wonderful Life, Brazil, The Conversation, Night of the Hunter, Blow-Up, Eraserhead, Ace in the Hole,* and *Citizen Kane.* And there are many more. What is most important is that these films had a vision and passion behind them, and the rules were being broken for specific reasons that define them as classics.

## VOICE-OVER

Part of breaking rules is the modern dislike of voice-over as a crutch. This technique is considered lazy writing because the writer has not done the hard work of telling the story through action and behavior. Often voice-over is used when the writers ideas aren't visual or those ideas require excessive exposition. It is the equivalent of creating a secondary character who has no place in the story except to listen to the main character's exposition.

There are many examples of stellar voice-over. In *Apocalypse Now,* the internal voice of Captain Willard works wonderfully. At times, this voice-over is giving us exposition as Willard reads through Kurtz's dossier, and at other times, Willard gives us his perspective on what he is experiencing. Elements of the themes come out of these observations. The important thing to keep in mind is that Willard's internal voice is a point of view and not a "voice of God." This isn't a "Once upon a time . . ." narration but a character who is sharing his experience through the expression of thoughts and feelings.

*Taxi Driver* is an ideal example of this. Travis Bickle is humanized as we see his world through his own point of view. Without this voice-over, the audience might not be able to associate and empathize with Travis and his condition. We are free to disagree with him even as we are allowed into his world to watch him go deeper and deeper into his own twisted morality.

*Double Indemnity* and *Sunset Boulevard* have crisp and entertaining voice-overs, although these would seem very old-fashioned in the modern day. *Double Indemnity* creates logic for the voice-over as Walter confesses to the insurance investigator, Keyes, by recording it into Keyes' Dictaphone. *Sunset Boulevard* is more unconventional, as Joe Gillis narrates his story from the grave. In the final version of the film, Gillis starts his narrative while floating face first in Norma Desmond's pool. In the initial script and production, the film starts in a morgue with Gillis and fellow corpses having a conversation in voice-over. Test audiences found the scene funny and Wilder, wanting a darker tone to start with, changed it to the swimming pool. The Gillis voice-over gives the audience a much more cynical point of view than if they told the story straight without it. Again, it employs a point of view where the audience is provided with character and emotional reaction as opposed to information (exposition).

John Duigan's *The Year My Voice Broke* and *Flirting* are perfect examples of voice-over used more for characterization than exposition. Noah Taylor's pitch perfect performance brings the audience into Danny Embling's world and to his point of view. It is a much more intimate and personal journey into the unique and vulnerable world of a young man growing up. Danny reacts to the situations he finds himself in and he reflects on them. This doesn't distract the viewer from the emotional elements of the film. The viewer experiences what Danny experiences and then gets a view into his perspective on it.

*To Kill a Mockingbird* employs a voice-over of an older person reflecting on her childhood. The advantage of this is that it gives meaning to the events of the film outside of the time of the film. Just as we reflect on our pasts and see how they shaped us, Scout reflects on her own life and an extraordinary moment in time. *Stand by Me* is another film that uses this technique, and if used properly this is effective. The voice-over isn't used to give information but to reveal character and theme.

The initial release of *Blade Runner* used voice-over narration that was subsequently dropped. The narration was added because the studio was concerned that the movie didn't make sense without it. Most fans of the film prefer not having the narrator, as it doesn't add much to the film, save for some needless exposition—the worst kind of voice-over.

One voice-over that I find unnecessary is found in Oliver Stone's *Platoon*. I admire Oliver Stone, and *Platoon* is a powerful film. But the voice-over seems irrelevant in terms of character development and exposition. Mostly it feels like Stone is doling out too much theme and hitting the nail on the head too hard. It works in *Apocalypse Now* because Willard is such a quiet and interior person that the audience does get a sense of his inner self. It also provides exposition about Kurtz through the dossiers that Willard is given at several points in the film. In *Platoon*, the device is used as Chris (Charlie Sheen) is writing letters to his Grandmother.

> *"Somebody once wrote Hell is the impossibility of Reason. That's what this place feels like. I hate it already and it's only been a week. Some goddamn week, grandma…"*

He goes on to describe his experiences as a new soldier, most of which the audience experiences in the film through the actions of the scenes. We experience the heat, mosquitoes and exhaustion. We experience the disdain that the experienced soldiers have for the rookies. The voice-over is redundant to the action of the film.

> *"'Course Mom and Dad didn't want me to come, they wanted me to be just like them - respectable, hardworking, making $200 a week, a little house, a family. They drove me crazy with their goddamn world, grandma, you know Mom, I don't want to be a white boy on Wall Street, I don't want my whole life to be predetermined by them."*

As far as character development goes, this is fairly slight, even if does come from Stone's own feelings as a young man. We find out early, through dialogue with other soldiers, that Chris volunteered for Vietnam and that he is a college boy who really should be an officer instead of a grunt. This character exposition seems to be unnecessary and adds very little to our understanding of Chris. It feels fairly generic, especially when you put it against Michael Herr's voice-over in *Apocalypse Now*. Michael Herr, the writer responsible for the great Vietnam book *Dispatches*, was brought in to write the voice-over for *Apocalypse*.

> *"When I was home after my first tour, it was worse. I'd wake up and there'd be nothing. I hardly said a word to my wife until I said yes to a divorce. When I was here, I wanted to be there. When I was there . . . all I could think of was getting back into the jungle. I'm here a week now. Waiting for a mission. Getting softer. Every minute I stay in this room, I get weaker. And every minute Charlie squats in the bush . . . he gets stronger. Each time I looked around . . . the walls moved in a little tighter."*

Willard, alone with his boredom, gives us a sense of his inner conflict. Unlike Chris, Captain Willard doesn't have other characters with whom he shares his thoughts or feelings. "Waiting for a mission" is the statement of his goal in the film. He gets his mission.

> *"Everyone gets everything he wants. I wanted a mission. And for my sins, they gave me one. Brought it up to me like room service."*

His mission (goal) is to go up the river, find Colonel Kurtz and assassinate him ("terminate with extreme prejudice").

*"New Year's Day, 1968. Just another day. Staying alive. There's been a lot of movement near the Cambodian border, regiments of NVA moving across. A lot of little firefights, ambushes, we drop a lot of bombs, then we walk through the napalm like ghosts in a landscape . . ."*

The line about walking "through the napalm like ghosts in a landscape" is evocative and poetic but doesn't add anything more to what the audience is already experiencing in the film. It doesn't reveal character, and the exposition about the Cambodian border isn't specific and could easily be put into the dialogue of the scenes.

*"We had to get to the village before dark so we left Elias with some men to keep looking and to wait for the engineers . . . But it was King who found him . . . about 1000 yards downriver, not far from the village – It was the end of the mystery."*

Again, there is nothing here that couldn't be done, or isn't done, through the action and dialogue of the scenes.

*"I think now, looking back, we did not fight the enemy, we fought ourselves – and the enemy was in us . . . The war is over for me now, but it will always be there – the rest of my days. As I am sure Elias will be – fighting with Barnes for what Rhah called possession of my soul . . . There are times since I have felt like the child born*

*of those two fathers . . . but be that as it may, those of us who did make it have an obligation to build again, to teach to others what we know and to try with what's left of our lives to find a goodness and meaning to this life . . ."*

Stone sums up his thematic approach to the film here, but it adds very little to the film as we "got it" while experiencing the film. We saw Barnes shoot Elias. We understand it through the action of the characters in the film.

I admire *Platoon*. It is a powerful film, and it is informed by Stone's real experiences as a soldier in Vietnam. The truth comes through our experience of the film and the voice-over doesn't add anything of value to that experience.

## TIME, SPACE AND THE ART OF EDITING—01.00.00.00

*"Carlyle said that almost everything examined deeply enough will turn out to be musical. Of course this is profoundly true of motion pictures. The pictures have movement; the movies move. Then there's the movement from one picture to another. There's a rhythmic structuring to that; there's counterpoint, harmony and dissonance. A film is never right, until it's right musically. This movieola, this filmmaker's tool, is a kind of a musical instrument." – Orson Welles*

There is a saying that editors make good directors—David Lean, Hal Ashby, and Robert Wise proved that. I put forward that good editors can make good writers as well. I have noticed that there are many film writers that have yet to make a film, and I think that is unfortunate. There is so much to be learned by shooting and editing a film that the film writer can better understand the medium and its possibilities. Is it any wonder that so many writer/directors have had such successes over the years? Coppola, Allen, Welles, Kieslowski, Kurosawa, Bergman, Fellini, Wilder, Huston, the Coen Brothers, Kubrick, Nolan—the list goes on. The more the writer understands the medium, the better he or she can write for it.

Time and space. Time is problematic for the film writer. Film is a time-based art and it exists as frames, seconds, and minutes. A painting or a photograph can be viewed at the leisure of the viewer. A novel will be read over the course of days or weeks. Film is viewed at the determined pace of the editing. The problem for the writer of films is that text is not based in time. We can read with leisure. Like a novel, we can pick up a text and put it down at will. We can tune out or skip forward to the next part of it or take a moment to consider what we've read. A screenplay starts as a timeless entity. Screenwriters have the unenviable task of having to try to imagine their ideas timed out to a merciless clock.

The writer becomes dependent on the director and performers and, in the end, the editor to make his or her vision work. The more the writer understands this, the better he or she will be able to craft the script to work more for the screen than the page.

William Goldman said that dialogue isn't the most important part of screenwriting but that structure is. What he meant was we are a slave to time and pace. Wilder said that screenplays were a mixture of "poetry and architecture." Our scripts need to have momentum, and we need to engage the audience from one moment to the next. This is where excellent screenwriters succeed. Whether they consciously understands it or not, excellent screenwriters write a compelling drama. They anticipate the audience's reaction and tightly control their expectations. This creates a wave that carries the audience forward. Excellent screenwriters engage us and challenge us. They make us care about the protagonist. They make us want to see the protagonist succeed.

I was having a conversation with a friend about the importance of a good editor in film and he seemed to think, in his experience, that picture editors were merely button pushers—technicians who ran the equipment. I was baffled by the conversation, particularly because I was talking to a fellow director.

It has been said many times that the writing team that makes up a film is the writer, the director, and the editor. Each person contributes to the story in very concrete ways. In the vaguest sense, the writer creates the scenario and dialogue and explores the themes of the piece. The director helps to further shape—the visual part of the story—and creates the tone and style as well as informing the performances. It is the editor's job to take all that has been designed and shot and shape it into a coherent piece. The editor becomes, as the famous editor Walter Murch puts it, the representative for the audience. The editor is not concerned with the writer or director's initial intentions, the editor is set to the task of making what was shot work for the film.

> *"The central occupation of the film editor, is to put himself/herself in place of the audience. What is the audience going to be thinking at any particular moment? Where are they going to be looking? What do you want them to think about? What do they need to think about? And, of course, what do you want them to feel? If you keep this in mind (and it's the preoccupation of every magician), then you are a kind of magician. Not in the supernatural sense, just an everyday, working magician."*
>
> *—Walter Murch*

As Welles alluded to earlier, the editor is not only creating the rhythm of the film, the editor is also trying to focus and control the story. Our enjoyment of a film story has so much to do with our experience of the film. This is where collaboration is the most effective. Sometimes the stars align and a film like *Casablanca* is born, and sometimes things fall out of synch and the film falls flat.

> *"For my style, for my vision of the cinema, editing is not simply one aspect: it is the aspect . . . The only time one is able to exercise control over the film is in the editing. The images themselves are not sufficient. They're very important, but they're only images. What's essential is the duration of each image and that which follows each image: the whole eloquence of cinema is that it's achieved in the editing room." – Orson Welles*

Anyone who has ever made a film understands that the moment you arrive at a location, you are at the mercy of time and circumstance. Everything on the face of the earth seems to come together to conspire against you. It is in the editing room that you start the film over again, throwing out all initial intentions and replacing them with the reality of what you shot. This isn't to say that the film is replaced, rather, it represents another opportunity to react to the story as it exists and to reshape it. Things you thought would work well fall flat, while things you struggled with come off as a smashing success.

Filmmaking is a collaborative art, and the process is one in which the film gets written many times before you end up with a finished print. There is give-and-take between the writer, the director, and the editor, and while the director gets the final say, the editor is integral to the process. A great editor is worth his or her weight in gold. Editors are that fresh set of eyes that helps to write the rhythm and tone (and sometimes structure) of the movie.

The writer is the originator of the ideas, plot, theme, characters and so much more. But in writing these things, there is a certain neglect of the aspect of time and the rhythmic musicality of the art of filmmaking. The film writer doesn't need to have directed or edited a film or television show, although it certainly helps. It helps you to understand the medium. It helps you understand what works and what does not work. It also informs you in a way that you might experiment with narrative and visual ideas. This isn't true for all writers of film but it sure helps.

Here is a small list of film directors who are or were editors:

Joel and Ethan Coen (under the pseudonym Roderick Jaynes)

James Cameron

Robert Wise

David Lean

Steven Soderbergh (under the pseudonym Mary Ann Bernard)

Robert Rodriguez

Hal Ashby

Akira Kurosawa

Orson Welles (uncredited on several films)

What is interesting about this small but distinguished list is that all of the directors named, with the exception of Robert Wise, are also writers. This isn't to say that you need to be a triple threat to be a great filmmaker, but it does show that filmmakers with a complete understanding of the medium of cinema are able to craft such memorable and important films. With an understanding of the craft of editing, the writer can write for the edit and can make that leap of imagination from words on a white page to moving images playing on a screen in real time.

## Screenplay Format

Novice film and television writers often go crazy trying to figure out screenplay formatting. They obsess and worry about it. It is true that good formatting is the sign of a professional writer, and you will be judged by a reader or producer if your work looks amateur.

What you need to understand is why a screenplay is formatted the way it is. A screenplay is not written to be read, it is written to be broken down into component pieces and filmed. Thus, all of the formatting that is done is for the sake of the crew and artists working on the film. The screenplay is broken down by all of the departments working on the film.

```
INT. FACTORY - DAY
```

For example, in the scene heading above, there is a call to action for many departments. The location is stated, which is of great interest to the location scout and production designer. Will this be built on a sound stage or will it be an existing location? The producer needs to know the locations to budget for it. The cinematographer needs to know what kind of lighting will be required. The production manager will look at how many scenes take place at the factory and determine how many days will be needed to get all of the shots done. These departments will spend months working out all the details that arise from a fairly simple scene header.

After the scene heading you can write your action. This is where you will describe what your characters are doing. Don't write camera moves. When someone writes, "dolly into his eyes and pan to the knife on the desk" the reader of the script is taken out of the film. They see a film crew on a dolly instead of the characters eyes and the knife.

The director will be the one to choose lenses, camera moves, and composition. Your job, as the writer, is to write the story. However, you make many suggestions to the director, as the above example shows. By capitalizing key elements, you, as the writer, highlight their importance and suggest the style of shooting and editing. Capitalizing a major prop also has the props people out searching for the ideal knife for the scene. By writing "His EYES," you are telling the director to shoot a close-up. The suggestion is there for how to shoot the scene, and it is much easier on the reader too.

Whenever I write action, I think of it like an editor in the editing suite. Think in *shots*. I don't mean angles or camera movement; think of each line in your script like a cut in the movie. I use my return key in my writing software the way I use the trim window on an Avid. This gives the screenplay a flow that is easy to read and easy to understand. I have read screenplays where the description is too dense. This might feel good to the writer, but it is easy to get bogged down trying to read it. Keep it simple and minimal. Get your ideas across clearly, and keep the narrative moving. Great artisans will riff off of what you have written, and they will do a spectacular job of it. If you give a clear and simple description of a location, the production designer will fill in the rest for you. You just need to give a clear direction of what is needed for the story.

Always capitalize the first time a character appears in the

film. This makes it easier for the casting department. One annoying thing I see all the time is when the writer starts off calling a character "The Man" or "The Woman" and then waits for their name to be spoken in the screenplay before changing it. Remember that your screenplay is meant to be played and not read. The casting department doesn't need to be confused and neither do your actors. Just name your characters from the start.

Here is an example of screenplay formatting:

```
INT. LOCATION - DAY

In this area we write the action. Be specific
but be sparse. No one wants to read long-
winded descriptions.

Note that if a HOUSE is a location, that
house can have several locations in it.
There might be a Kitchen, Living Room,
Bathroom and Bedroom. You will need to
differentiate these so the script can be
broken down efficiently. This is to say that
all of the Kitchen scenes will be shot on
one day and all of the Bedroom shots would
be shot on another. The production manager
will try to group as many single locations
as possible in order to limit the amount of
lighting changes and Camera setups.

In terms of writing action, even if it is a
fight scene, write it sparse. You might say
they exchange blows or that punches and
kicks are thrown. Avoid detailed choreography
as they'll hire a professional to do that.

Once you've established your action and
introduce a CHARACTER you can write the
dialogue.

                    CHARACTER

This is where the characters witty and
important dialogue is written. They might
```

> do something important or another
> CHARACTER might appear in the film.

CHARACTER 2

There is an exchange of dialogue. Character 2 wants something from Character.

CHARACTER

(Parenthetical)

The parenthetical isn't for action but small nuances in the reading of a line.

CHARACTER 2

(Grins)

If you want to ensure that the line is being read as ironic or otherwise you should use a parenthetical. Use it sparingly, as it is to the actor as writing camera direction is to the director, annoying.

A third character may call out from a different room.

CHARACTER 3 (O.S.)

This means Off Screen. You might see it written as (O.O.V) as well. This means Out of View.

Use (O.S.) when the characters are in the same physical space but in different rooms or areas. This helps to determine who needs to be on Set on the shooting day.

CHARACTER 2 (V.O.)

If your script requires a Voice Over than this is how you would write it. You might also use (V.O.) if a character is talking to another on the telephone.

All of this helps to breakdown what is needed for the shooting days. If the character is talking on the telephone to a minor character, then the director or another actor on the set might feed the lines and save having to pay another actor for a days work that isn't required.

All of this comes out of your script, so if you get confused about some formatting then think about who is breaking it down and what they need to know from your script.

The best thing you can do is to purchase screen writing software, or take advantage of some of the free software available. It allows you to write quickly without worrying about the specific spacing and formatting requirements.

If you are not computer savvy, you can also write with pen and paper. Eventually it will need to be typed out if you are sending it anywhere, but pen and paper works perfectly fine to get your screenplay started.

"The Third Man *was never written to be read but only to be seen. . . . To me it is almost impossible to write a film play without first writing a story. Even a film depends on more than plot, on a certain measure of characterization, on mood and atmosphere; and these seem to me almost impossible to capture for the first time in the dull shorthand of a script. One can reproduce an effect caught in another medium, but one cannot make the first act of creation in script form. One must have the sense of more material than one needs to draw on." – Graham Greene*

Graham Greene was a famous English novelist who was no stranger to the movies. Many of his books and short stories have been translated to film, and he had a hand in a few of them: *The Fallen Idol, Brighton Rock, Our Man in Havana,* and the classic *The Third Man.* What's interesting about *The Third Man* is that it was imagined and written directly for the screen. It was not an adaptation of previous work. Greene says that he wrote the idea down on an envelope.

> *"I had paid my last farewell to Harry a week ago, when his coffin was lowered into the frozen February ground, so that it was with incredulity that I saw him pass by, without a sign of recognition, among the host of strangers in the Strand."*

Greene couldn't write in the "dull shorthand of a script." He ended up writing the story first as a novella then adapted it to a screenplay (he refers to the novella as a treatment). Greene understood that writing full and rounded characters was not the strength of the screenplay. Characterization in movies tends to be thin, as we mostly judge a character by what they do. Writing a novella first allowed Greene to work out past histories and backstory and to give an inner voice to his main character, Rollo Martins.

The screenplay format does make the reading of the story much less appealing and, as stated before, it is really a technical document meant for production. Whereas Greene preferred to write the story as prose first, other film writers have all sorts of techniques to try to fill out characters and ideas.

Some writers create character biographies that allow them to explore backstory and character traits outside of the film. There is software that allows you to analyze your script and your dramatic structure. Again, whatever works for you is fine. For the great Graham Greene, it was writing the film as a short story first.

As a digression, Greene does note that the famous Cuckoo Clock dialogue was written by Orson Welles, as the scene needed another beat before Harry Lime, played by Welles, took his leave.

> *"You know what the fellow said—in Italy, for thirty years under the Borgias, they had warfare, terror, murder and bloodshed, but they produced Michelangelo, Leonardo da Vinci and the Renaissance. In Switzerland, they had brotherly love, they had five hundred years of democracy and peace—and what did that produce? The cuckoo clock."*

What is funny is that this is all merely historically reputed. The Swiss never made Cuckoo Clocks, and during the Borgias, the Swiss were a major military force. It is still memorable—and memorable in the context of the scene. Harry and Holly (Greene changed the name from Rollo to an American named Holly) have had their first confrontation on the Riesenrad Ferris Wheel, a Vienna attraction to this day. There is strong tension in the scene and there is hint that Harry might just kill Holly and throw him off the cabin to the ground below. Harry eventually withdraws, and on leaving the scene tries to find some levity and moral exoneration with Welles's added lines, and thus a great bit of dialogue is created.

## THE SHAWSHANK REDEMPTION

What an odd success this film became. Upon release, the film didn't even make its budget back, but like *It's a Wonderful Life*, *The Shawshank Redemption* found an audience on television and home video. As I write this, it currently stands as the one of the highest rated films on the Internet Movie Database. This upsets film purists who cannot conceive that this little prison movie would be held in higher esteem than *The Godfather, The Bicycle Thief, Vertigo,* and *Citizen Kane* (and this list goes on). Certainly the IMDB list doesn't reflect the critical establishment, but it does tell us that people love this movie. Why?

One of the reasons the film didn't do well theatrically may have been because it was a prison movie with a running time of over two hours. This doesn't exactly scream "date movie" or invite the female audience to want to come out. Furthermore, it didn't have any big name stars and had very little action. How does someone market a film with little action, no love story, and no stars?

Prison films, like courtroom dramas, and war films have built in drama. The stakes are usually life or death, and there is plenty of danger. At the beginning of *Shawshank,* we learn that Andy Dufresne (Tim Robbins) has been convicted of murdering his wife and her lover. Andy is shown preparing for murder as he sits in his car with a bottle of whiskey, loading a gun. We don't see him commit the crime, instead we cut back and forth to the court room where Andy is sentenced to life in prison.

In terms of goals, the prison film is a simple and straight-forward narrative. The protagonist must survive the other prisoners and guards. The second goal is to prove his innocence or escape the prison. Either way, it is a clean line of action and a simple, but dramatic, setup.

Frank Darabont's adaptation of Stephen King's novella *Rita Hayworth and Shawshank Redemption* is unique because it breaks the conventions of the sub-genre of prison films. There are things we expect to happen in a prison film, such as the violence of the inmates and the ever present threat of rape. These things are in the film. Where Darabont's script becomes unique is in the point of view. The audience has a sense that the protagonist of the film is Andy Dufresne, but Andy is quiet and introspective. Instead Darabont makes Red (Morgan Freeman) the central character of the film, giving him the voice-over narration and the main point of view. What is fascinating here is that this technique, combined with Andy's sparse dialogue, creates a mystique around Andy. He is a mystery, and we rarely know what he is thinking and are often surprised by his actions.

Let us take a closer look at the story by breaking it down into its component parts.

<u>The Characters:</u>

Red: When creating memorable characters, we try to find something extraordinary about them. As for Red, he can get you anything you need in prison. If you need a bottle of whiskey or a poster of Rita Hayworth, Red is your man. In prison, he is an important man. His goal in the film is to bide his time and gain his freedom. We first meet him at a parole board hearing where his parole is rejected. His greatest fear is becoming institutionalized, which is a central theme of the film. The casting of Morgan Freeman was spot on because he brings weight and class to the role.

Andy: Andy Dusfresne is a quiet and crafty character. He doesn't say much, but there is a sense that he is always thinking. His extraordinary quality is his intelligence and his way with money. This puts him into favor with the Warden, when he is called in to cook the books and cover up the corruption of the prison officials. It is not good enough for Andy to have been a good banker; he proves to the best. Andy's goal is survival and at the end of the film, we discover, to escape. Andy is a gentle soul. He is generous and bullish in his determination.

In an ensemble piece you can have multiple protagonists, and while I wouldn't call *The Shawshank Redemption* "ensemble," I would put forward that Red and Andy are both the protagonists of the story. They are two pieces of the whole. The audience identifies with both of them.

What I find interesting about prison films is that the audience will empathize with your characters, even though they wouldn't want real life convicts coming over for dinner. The audience can identify with Red, as he seems to be reformed and wise from his years in prison. They identify with Andy because they believe that he has been wrongly convicted. The audience empathizes even more with Andy because he is kind and generous. He barters for beers for his fellow convicts when they are tasked with tarring the roof of the License Plate Factory. Through dogged determination, he builds a proper prison library and helps his fellow inmates get their high school equivalency. He seems selfless.

<u>The Archetypes:</u>

Most of the remaining characters in the film are based on archetypes and cast with strong character actors.

Warden Norton: The Warden is a corrupt and unsympathetic man. He is harsh and unyielding. He is the most egregious of hypocrites, preaching the Bible on one hand and laundering money with the other.

Captain Hadley: Hadley is a cruel and brutal prison guard. He poses as much a threat to Andy as do the other inmates. He is sadistic in doling out punishment.

Bogs Diamond: Bogs is the central antagonist for the first half of the film. He and his gang called "the Sisters" prey on Andy, submitting him to beatings and rape.

These three men are all antagonists in various parts of the story. All three fall into the category of archetypes because there isn't anything redeemable or complicated about them. There are no shades of gray in these characters, and when they are an ally to Andy, it is only because Andy is providing them with a service. They cut him slack when it is in their own interest.

The remaining characters are colored in with what you have come to expect from prison movies (the old bird man and the wisecracker). These aren't bad things but are a necessary part of making movies. There is an element of shorthand at work when dealing with minor characters in film, and archetypes and good casting help to bring them to life so the audience can quickly associate those characters to their archetypal roles. The novelist might have an opportunity to give some backstory or fill these characters out, but in a film, you need to keep the narrative moving.

Darabont does do a little bit of invention in the adaptation by creating the character of Brooks. Brooks is the oldest resident of the prison. He is "the Birdman" of the film, who has spent his life in the prison. He is soft spoken and gentle, and he becomes the personification of one of the themes of the film. This idea of "institutionalization," where men replace hope with comfort. Brooks is comfortable in the prison. He works the prison library and is "family" with Red and his community of inmates. When Brooks is granted parole, Darabont does an interesting thing by following him out into the world. The voice-over that was exclusively Red's is now taken over by Brooks, and Darabont explores the thematic ideas of the film. Brooks, alone and without hope for a future, commits suicide. Brooks may have been free in the form of his body, but he wasn't free in his mind. This episode is a form of digression from the main story, but Darabont makes it work through the voice-over narration and because of the audience's genuine love of Brooks as a character, as played by actor James Whitmore. Casting is key for roles like these, and Whitmore embodies that character perfectly, thus allowing for Darabont to change of point of view and a digress from the main thrust of the film. It is daring to depart from your principle characters to follow the side story of a minor character. Darabont pulls it off.

The Structure:

*The Shawshank Redemption* doesn't have a clearly defined line of action. Survival is the main stay of the prison film, but eventually the audience wants to know where it is going. The first half of the film relies on the goal of survival.

Structurally the film works episodically. It is unusual that a film's story would take place over a twenty year period, and it is obvious that a clean line of action isn't going to work. An episodic structure allows us to experience the film in vignettes. These vignettes are connected, but in order for it to work within a two-hour running time, there needs to be some forward momentum. You can skip from one short vignette to the other, but eventually the audience wants to feel like the story is leading somewhere. There are many satisfying twists of plot in the film, but how do you turn the film in the direction of a satisfying resolution? This is where Tommy comes in. Tommy is a small-time crook with a lot of swagger but not much sense. He is young and foolish, and he is eventually taken in by Andy, who is determined to help him get his high school equivalency and to send him out of the prison with the skills to survive as an honest man. Tommy provides a fresh injection of character into the film, but more importantly, he advances the plot by telling Andy the story of a convict who confessed to a murder of a woman and her golf pro lover. This new turn of events propels the story forward, as this seems to be the key to proving Andy's innocence. The audience now has a clean line of action and a renewed sense of where the story is leading. What is stopping Andy from getting what he wants?

This proof of innocence? The Warden becomes the main antagonist at this point of the story. Not only does Andy have all the dirt on the Warden's illegal activities, he is also the brilliant accountant who makes sure that those activities stay unnoticed. In other words, the Warden needs Andy, and any talk of innocence stands in the way of what the Warden wants. His goal is to maintain the status quo. As a result, Tommy is murdered, and the Warden punishes Andy to send a clear message; he is not getting out of prison as an innocent man.

In the push to the resolution of the film, the audience wants to know what is going to happen next. How will Andy prove his innocence? And how will the film end in a way that will satisfy the audience? Darabont does a little magic trick, in which he echoes Brooks's suicide and gets the audience feeling that there is no more hope for Andy. It seems that Andy is going to give into his darker self and end his own life.

The twist:

In the end, the audience learns that Andy did indeed have a clean line of action after all. Right under the nose of his friends —and the audience—he has spent the better part of twenty years digging his way to freedom. The audience can cheer at this point because they are sure of his innocence and have seen the injustice of the prison Warden. It is okay for us to root for Andy.

Red is finally paroled, and the audience doesn't want to see Red go the way of Brooks. They want to know that things will turn out better for him. The idea of hope is confirmed when Red and Andy are reunited again as free men.

The Theme:

There are many reasons that *The Shawshank Redemption* has become an audience favorite since its release in 1994, and one of the main reasons is theme. Frank Darabont, as writer and director, always focuses the story on theme. This is why a film can be viewed multiple times by an audience. The audience finds the film a great metaphor for their lives. This theme is stated many times in the film and it drives the narrative.

*"Let me tell you something my friend. Hope is a dangerous thing. Hope can drive a man insane."* – *Red*

*"These walls are funny. First you hate 'em, then you get used to 'em. Enough time passes, you get so you depend on them. That's institutionalized."* – *Red*

*"Remember, Red, hope is a good thing, maybe the best of things, and no good thing ever dies."* – *Andy*

*"I find I'm so excited, I can barely sit still or hold a thought in my head. I think it's the excitement only a free man can feel, a free man at the start of a long journey whose conclusion is uncertain. I hope I can make it across the border. I hope to see my friend and shake his hand. I hope the Pacific is as blue as it has been in my dreams. I hope."* – *Red*

*"Get busy living, or get busy dying."* – *Andy*

There is so much to appreciate about Frank Darabont's adaptation of Stephen King's novel. Theme is the thing that ties it all together. It is the guiding element throughout the story. He keeps coming back to this idea of hope and the inner strength to find one's own way in life. And audience reacted positively to it. Similarly, in *It's a Wonderful Life*, Frank Capra convinces the audience that life is worth living if you live it well and with purpose. Both films have unusual structures, but both films connect to the audience on a deeper level. Theme takes the story beyond a good yarn and gives it more meaning.

I admire *The Shawshank Redemption*, even if it isn't on my list of top films. It is fascinating how the film struck a chord in the modern audience's imagination and it is important to deconstruct it to see how and why.

### Craft and Collaboration.

The craftsmanship of this film is another reason why the film is so successful. The lighting and photography of Roger Deakins is perfect. The tone of the film is perfectly set by composer Thomas Newman. The score veers away from melodrama and provides a depth of emotion that underscores the drama. The film's editor, Richard Francis-Bruce, is sure handed in the pacing and control of the film. Production design, wardrobe, and art direction make us believe that we are in this time in America. The casting is perfect and the performances are powerful.

It all starts with a great story by Stephen King and a brilliant adaptation by Frank Darabont. The translation from the text to the screen is unconventional and so confident and assured.

You can say that the film is a bit sentimental and earnest. I would say the same thing about *It's a Wonderful Life*. Both films avoid being pulled down by this sentimentality because they are anchored by strong thematic content and great characters.

In terms of "cinema," *The Shawshank Redemption* is an accessible and uplifting film, and it is easy to see why it is so popular. The themes feel "universal" and the twists of plot are exciting and unexpected. Darabont hit all the right notes making the film, and it is clear why it endures. Why it is #1 on the IMDB list is still a mystery, but I suppose something has to be.

## HOW TO MAKE A MILLION DOLLARS

Rather than try my hand at being a snake oil salesman, I will tell you there is no "formula" for selling your scripts and making millions of dollars. There are plenty of books that will tell you how to write for the marketplace, and if that is your interest, then go for it. My only problem with "the marketplace" is that it is a dynamic and fluid beast. Predicting the market is a bit like predicting the weather or the stock market. The film and television market might have trends that will run their course, but no one knows when that will happen. Any student of film history can see this happen in the transition of the old studio moguls to the corporate control of the film business in the 1960s and 1970s. When you consider that George Lucas secured the toy rights for *Star Wars*, you can see that the powers-that-be can overlook something that was a mega-money maker. Yes, they learned from that mistake, but there are plenty of mistakes yet to be made.

Consider the huge success of *Harry Potter* and *The Lord of the Rings*. In the past, Hollywood would stay far away from fantasy properties, as they were marginal successes with a limited audience. Or so Hollywood thought. No one could have predicted the runaway success of J. K. Rowling's *Harry Potter* books and this, like *Star Wars*, proved that there was an audience for good fantasy and science fiction. Will the trend last? Probably not. As Wilder says, "the audience is fickle." The trends will shift unexpectedly, and there will be a new culling of studio executives and marketing people.

*The Pirates of the Caribbean* was another series that proved there could be an appetite for pirate movies. After the disaster of *Cutthroat Island*, the conventional wisdom became "pirate movies don't do business." This isn't true, and the mantra should now be "*bad* Pirate movies don't do business". Good movies generally do good business. Not all good movies mind you. We already talked about *The Shawshank Redemption* flopping at the box office. You can also include Brian Depalma's *Blow Out* and Brad Bird's wonderful classically animated adaptation of *The Iron Giant*. Peter Weir's excellent film *Master and Commander* didn't do great business at the box office despite the star power of Russell Crowe. However, most good films that don't have a strong showing at the box office still go on to find an audience through television, home video, and streaming. Word of mouth is a significant tool, and those forgotten treasures usually have a way of having a long shelf life. *A Christmas Story* is another great example of this, as is *It's a Wonderful Life*.

The best advice I have to offer is to write something that is meaningful for you. Keep it personal. *E.T.* was a personal film, as was *Titanic*. These films were born out of passion and love. Even Guillermo del Toro's *Hellboy* films came from a place of passion and del Toro describes them as "personal films." Write the films that you want to see as if you are the audience you want. Writing for the market waters down a personal vision. There may be times that you take an assignment, but it is up to you to find your way into the material. Francis Coppola did this with *The Godfather*. He found what was personal and of interest to him.

Also remember that failure and frustration come with the territory. Success often happens with perseverance. If you write a film or television show that doesn't sell, move on to your next script. Your project may not be commercial enough or relevant at the moment. It might not be very good. It is hard to tell when you are so close to it. Just remember that rejection is the natural state of things, and you will be in good company.

Margaret Mitchell's book *Gone With the Wind* was reportedly rejected by 38 publishers. Of course it went on to be a best-selling novel and one of cinema's highest grossing films.

J. K. Rowling's *Harry Potter and the Philosopher's Stone* was rejected by twelve publishers. It too went on to become a phenomenal hit with successful films to follow.

John Grisham's first novel was repeatedly rejected by agents and publishers. Adaptations of his books have gone on to make many people rich.

Stephen King was no stranger to rejection, as he states in his book *On Writing:* "By the time I was fourteen . . . the nail in my wall would no longer support the weight of the rejection slips impaled upon it. I replaced the nail with a spike and kept on writing."

On the list of films that had a hard time finding financing are *Pulp Fiction, Star Wars, Raiders of the Lost Ark, American Graffiti, Back to the Future* and *E.T.* We are not talking about art house movies but films with commercial value that went on to phenomenal financial and critical success. All of these films were backed by passionate filmmakers who were determined to tell their stories. The rounds of rejection cannot stifle the passion of the writer, so when you get your rejections you can put the script in the drawer and start on your next.

For me, the process of writing the film is and should be the reward. My first draft is my own and in my mind it is a movie. If it doesn't sell, move on. Your writing will only get better.

# About the Author

Mark Achtenberg has spent his life confusing producers and potential employers. His resume includes working at a Psychiatric Institution, Public and College Libraries, The Canadian Air Force as well as a Student Journalist and Editor. He also grifted for the Coles book store in Toronto and has taught writing, editing and visual effects at Humber College and has lectured and given student feedback at the prestigious Sheridan College Animation school.

When he eventually shook off his past careers, Mark settled into working in the Film and Television industry. He has worked as a writer, director, editor and visual effects artist in animation and live action. Mark has continued his career in the exploration of film and is an avid student of all things that involve moving pictures. And in the interest of dropping names, Mark has worked on shows for Warner Brothers, Nickelodeon, Disney, BBC, CBC, Jim Henson Company, TVO, PBS, MTV and many others.

Needless to say, Mark loves stories. Like that time he got his boss out of jail. True story. Or another boss who should have gone to jail—true story for another day.

Mark currently lives in Whitby, Ontario in the Greater Toronto Area.

# Works Cited and Consulted

*Apocalypse Now*. Dir. Francis Coppola. By John Milius. Omni-Zoetrope, 1979. Transcript.

Behance, Inc. "Francis Ford Coppola: On Risk, Money, Craft & Collaboration." *99U by Behance*. Will Allen, Publisher, 07 Mar. 2016. Web.

Bricknell, Timothy, and Sydney Pollack. *Minghella on Minghella*. N.p.: Faber and Faber, 2005. Print.

"The Cask of Amontillado." *Full Text of "The Cask of Amontillado"*. The Project Gutenberg, n.d. Web.

*Filming Othello by Orson Welles*. Dir. Orson Welles. Produced by Klaus Hellwig, Juergen Hellwig, 1978. Transcript.

*Frozen*. Screenplay by Jennifer Lee. Disney/Pixar, 2014. Transcript.

Greene, Graham, and Carol Reed. *The Third Man*. N.p.: Faber and Faber, 1991. Print.

Greene, Graham. *The Third Man*. N.p.: Easy Readers, 1968. Print.

Kieslowski, Krzysztof, and Krzysztof Piesiewicz. *Dekalog*. N.p.: Jacek Santorski, 1996. Print.

Mamet, David. *Bambi vs. Godzilla on the Nature, Purpose, and Practice of the Movie Business*. N.p.: Pocket, 2008. Print.

Murch, Walter. *In the Blink of an Eye a Perspective on Film Editing*. N.p.: Silman-James, 2001. Print.

*Platoon*. Dir. Oliver Stone. An Orion Pictures Release, 1986. Transcript.

*The Shawshank Redemption*. Dir. Frank Darabont. Castle Rock
  Entertainment, 2004. Transcript.

Wilder, Billy, Cameron Crowe, and Karen Lerner.
  *Conversations with Wilder*. N.p.: Knopf, 2001. Print.

www.ingramcontent.com/pod-product-compliance
Lightning Source LLC
Chambersburg PA
CBHW032253070726
47590CB00016B/2613